9 in 9

NINE LIFE LESSONS LEARNED FROM PLAYING NINE POSITIONS IN ONE NINE INNING BASEBALL GAME

Published by BookLocker.com, Inc., Bradenton, Florida.

Printed in the United States of America.

BookLocker.com, Inc.
2013

FedEx®, FedEx Express®, FedEx Ground® and FedEx Freight® are registered trademarks of the Federal Express Corporation.

First Edition

DEDICATION

I would like to dedicate this book to anyone who has a dream and has the passion and courage to pursue it. Don't ever let anyone tell you that you can't do something. If your dream is to become a doctor, go and do it. If your dream is to become a lawyer, by all means go and do it. If your dream is to become a professional athlete, go and do it. Create the future that you want for yourself and go live it.

I would also like to dedicate this book to all of the people who may have doubted me in my life. I sincerely appreciate it, and I mean that. I wouldn't be where I am today without the motivation you provided me. To the people out there with doubters, use them as motivation to achieve your dreams. There's no better motivation in the world than trying to prove people wrong.

ACKNOWLEDGMENTS

The making of this book would not be possible without all of the amazing people in my life. I would like to first thank my parents and my family for always being there to support me through the good times as well as the rough times.

I would like to thank Jack Dahm, Nick Zumsande, and Ryan Brownlee for giving me the opportunity to play Division I Baseball at the University of Iowa. I would like to thank Steve Abney, Travis Fryman, Edwin Rodriguez and the entire Cleveland Indians Organization for giving me the opportunity to achieve a dream and assist me in playing professional baseball.

I would also like to thank Brian Cain for all of the valuable life lessons he has taught me over the years. Also, I would not be anywhere near where I am today without the many teammates and coaches I have had throughout my career. Whether it was in high school, college, or professionally, I could not have asked for a better group of guys to chase my dreams with.

I would also like to say thanks to anyone else out there who's made a positive impact on my life. I wouldn't be who I am today without the support and impact you've had on my life. Last but not least, a big thank you to everyone who helped out in the process of making this book a reality.

DISCLAIMER

This book details the author's personal experiences with and opinions based on his professional baseball career and knowledge of sports psychology. The author is not a licensed sports psychologist, he is merely speaking on behalf of the knowledge he has gained throughout his real world life and athletic experiences during his baseball career.

The author and publisher are providing this book and its contents on an "as is" basis and make no representations or warranties of any kind with respect to this book or its contents. The author and publisher disclaim all such representations and warranties, including for example warranties of merchantability for a particular purpose. In addition, the author and publisher do not represent or warrant that the information accessible via this book is accurate, complete or current.

The statements made about products and services have not been evaluated by the U.S. government. Please consult with your own legal or accounting professional regarding the suggestions and recommendations made in this book.

Except as specifically stated in this book, neither the author or publisher, nor any authors, contributors, or other representatives will be liable for damages arising out of or in connection with the use of this book. This is a comprehensive limitation of liability that applies to all damages of any kind, including (without limitation) compensatory; direct, indirect or consequential damages; loss of data, income or profit; loss of or damage to property and claims of third parties.

You understand that this book is not intended as a substitute for consultation with a licensed medical, legal or accounting professional. Before you begin any change your lifestyle in any way, you will consult a licensed professional to ensure that you are doing what's best for your situation.

This book provides content related to baseball, athletics, and sports psychology. As such, use of this book implies your acceptance of this disclaimer.

CONTENTS

FORWARD

I have had the pleasure of working with Justin as his mental conditioning coach since he was in college at the University of Iowa. I've gotten to know Justin as a player on the field and as a person off the field. The reason he has gotten where he has in his career is because of the things he talks about in this book.

Having watched Justin play, he isn't a super naturally talented athlete, but the reason he succeeds is because of his preparation, hard work, and his mental mindset. He has taken advantage of the opportunities he has been presented with and has a strong belief in his abilities as a player and in himself as a person.

As a teacher and master of the mental game, I have watched many athletes take their game to a new level as a result of proper mental training. Justin is no exception. I think he would agree that when he changed the way he thought about things and took interest in the mental game, his career took off.

Take advantage of the lessons Justin shares with you in this book. Control what you can control, take advantage of your opportunities, believe in yourself, be comfortable being uncomfortable, stay in the moment, and play pitch to pitch. Take advantage of the inexpensive experience he has shared with you in this book and use it in your own life.

- Brian Cain
Brian Cain Peak Performance

AUTHOR'S NOTE

The purpose of me writing this book is to challenge the people who read it. I challenge you to think outside of the box and view things you may think of as impossible as possible. In writing this book I wanted to talk about some of the things I have learned that have made a huge impact on my life, not only as an athlete, but as a person, and share them with you.

I had an opportunity to play nine positions in one game for the Carolina Mudcats, a minor league affiliate of the Cleveland Indians, during the 2012 season. In thinking about that game, I couldn't help but think about all of the lessons, struggles, ups, and downs I had experienced in my career that allowed me to accomplish that feat. Each little bump in the road, each roadblock I ran into, everything I experienced in one way or another shaped me into the player that allowed me to play a new position each inning on that day.

I hope you find this book to be inspirational and entertaining at the same time. I talk about the nine inning game and parallel it with many of my life experiences in hopes that you can use them as motivation that can hopefully make a difference in your life or someone's life you know. My goal wasn't to brag or talk myself up, but instead to share my experiences and accomplishments with you in hopes you can relate to those situations with experiences to situations you have encountered in your life.

My message for you, as you will see in this book, is to follow your dreams and take advantage of your opportunities. Don't let anyone tell you that you can't do something. If you have the will do to something, you can find a way to accomplish it.

Feel Free To Contact Me -
Email: Tooleyj24@yahoo.com
Follow me on Twitter: Tooleyj24

9 in 9

Chapter 1
Patience

"He that can have patience can have what he will."
- Benjamin Franklin

"The two most powerful warriors are patience and time."
— Leo Nikolaevich Tolstoy

The day I had long waited for was finally here. At the beginning of the season my manager, Edwin Rodriguez, told me that if I hadn't moved up and was still with his team at the end of the season, I would get a chance to play 9 different positions in one 9 inning game. Being a utility guy, I thought that would be pretty cool, but I didn't really think too much of it other than that. If I was around at the end of the season I'd worry about it when that time came, but until then I had some work to do.

As the season went along I found myself on a few different teams within the organization. I was called up to AAA Columbus early in the season and then again for a short stint in the middle of the season. On both occasions I returned back to High-A Carolina. I was also called up to AA Akron for what I figured to be the rest of the season in late July only to return back to Carolina a few weeks later in the middle of August. Everyone's goal in the minor leagues is to make it to the Major Leagues, so each time you move up you're really excited, but then when you get sent down it can be really tough. I looked at both getting called up and getting sent back as opportunities. Now that I was back in Carolina, I had an opportunity to accomplish something not many people at the professional level ever have the chance to do.

Pre-game was normal like always, except for my pre-game interview with our radio guy, Darren Headrick. The interview was to be played on the video board before the start of the game. The interview gave fans a heads up as to what was going to happen in the game. At the same time, I was able to let my thoughts and feelings out about how I thought the game was going to go. To be honest I don't know what was better, the questions Darren asked or the answers I gave him. This interview completely set the tone for me on this night. I knew it was going to be enjoyable not only for me, but for my teammates, everyone involved with the Carolina Mudcats, everyone involved with the Cleveland Indians, as well as all of the fans in attendance. I was definitely excited and ready to enjoy the experience.

The game started out just like any other game on any other ordinary evening. It was a typical Saturday night in Zebulon, North Carolina. The stands were filling up and there was a touch of fall in the air. On this night we were to take the field at Five County Stadium and square off against the Boston Red Sox Carolina League Affiliate, the Salem Red Sox. As the starting lineups were introduced, I took my place towards the top step of the dugout, eagerly waiting to take the field. As I was announced, hitting in the two spot, I took off from the dugout and made my way toward the middle of the diamond, toward my regularly played positions on the infield dirt. Everything was normal, except this time I didn't stop on the dirt. I continued into center field and took my spot for the National Anthem as the starting rightfielder for the Carolina Mudcats.

I warmed up throwing with our centerfielder, Delvi Cid, and my thoughts and emotions were racing. You name an emotion and I probably had it. I really didn't have much in terms of expectations heading into the night, but there were a few things I wanted to accomplish. I wanted to get a hit, I wanted to play good defense without committing an error, and most of all I wanted to win the game. I couldn't wait to call my parents, friends, and everybody else and tell them about all the cool things that had happened in the game. I didn't want to get ahead of myself, but I also couldn't wait to get the show on the road. If there was ever a time in my life I needed a little patience it was now. Throughout my life and my baseball career my patience has been tested quite a bit (probably too many times to be honest). As a result, I learned that a little patience can go a long way.

Not being an everyday outfielder, I didn't have my own outfielder's glove. In past years I always borrowed one from a teammate who I replaced in the lineup or from someone who had an extra one. In baseball, each person breaks in their own glove in a different way, and so it's sometimes kind of tricky to find one that you can use and are also comfortable with at the same time. I've been fortunate enough to have teammates like Donnie Webb, Tyler Holt, and on this particular night, Todd Hankins, who have at one time or another let me use their glove. Lucky for me, Todd was playing in the infield when I was in the outfield tonight, so I was able to use his outfield glove for the first three innings. To top it all off, it was a red and black Carolina Mudcats themed glove, so obviously I had to use it!

The first inning started well. The first hitter for Salem, Lucas LeBlanc, popped out to our first baseman Tyler Cannon. The next hitter, James Kang, singled up the middle. Michael Almanzar followed with a hard hit ball that was snagged by Hankins at third base. There were two outs and Kang was on first base when Brandon Jacobs struck out to end the inning. Just like that, the top of the first was over. I thought it would be cool to make a play at each position, but the top of the first quickly squashed any hopes of that. After the last out, I made my way back to our home dugout, located on the third base line. For those of you who are unfamiliar with baseball, the right field to third base dugout run and the left field to first base dugout run are the absolute worst. I don't think you will ever find an outfielder who would ever tell you he enjoyed doing either of those runs. Luckily for me I only had to do it once.

Standing in right field during the top half of the first inning and not getting any action allowed time for my mind to race with all kinds of thoughts and emotions. I was so anxious for the night to be over and for the game to be finished. I wished I could do something to speed the game up, but I realized I didn't actually have much control over how fast the game would go. Baseball is a grind with games usually lasting several hours. I just hoped that tonight's game would be a quick one.

Having played baseball for many years, I have experienced quick games, like pitching in a seven inning pitcher's duel in high school against Carroll Kuemper, a game that lasted just a little over an hour. I have also experienced long games, like the grind that is playing the entire game at third base in a twenty-three inning, six hour and twenty-seven minute game in Kinston, North Carolina in 2011. For the record, we were victorious in that game, 3-2, against the Texas Rangers Affiliate, the Myrtle Beach Pelicans. Although I had many years of baseball playing experience, I still needed patience and a deep breath to make it through this night.

Patience is something that I have never really had in my life. Anyone who knows me personally knows that I am an immediate results kind of person, even when it's probably not even reasonable. I was the kid growing up who when you gave me something to do, I focused on the end result, the whole thing being done, and would do it as fast as I possibly could. It didn't matter how I got to the end of what I was doing as long as I was the first one to do so. I was "that" kid growing up. It wasn't until I got older that I realized life is not about the outcome, but rather it's about the process. I couldn't always get the results I desired overnight. Whether it was on the soccer field, the basketball court, the football field, the baseball diamond, or the classroom, I had to have patience. Tonight was no different; I couldn't just focus on the end result of playing all nine positions in nine innings. Instead, I had to have patience and focus on playing the game one pitch at a time.

During my senior year of high school I wasn't sure where my baseball career was going to take me. I had a number of Division 1 baseball schools interested in me, but I wasn't for sure where I was going to end up. Anyone who has ever gone through the recruiting process knows the kind of headache it can be. One school may like you, another one might not. One school might sign someone and tell you they don't think they have room for you while another school might lose a recruit and suddenly gain a huge interest in you. I immediately learned that I needed to have patience and let things play out.

Most athletes sign in the fall signing period, while many others sign in the spring. I did neither. I waited, and by no means by choice, until I had actually graduated from high school before I made my college decision. Early on in the recruiting process I had a few junior college scholarships, a couple Division II offers, but none from Division I schools. I was dead set on going to a D-I school but I didn't have any scholarship offers. In order to get one, I had to have patience. Eventually, in the spring of my senior year, I finally got the offers I had long waited for. I had been in contact with schools like Nebraska, Creighton, Minnesota, Kansas State, Northern Iowa, Northern Illinois, Iowa, along with Nebraska Omaha, Iowa Western Community College, and Indian Hills Community College. Some eventually offered scholarships, while others offered walk-on deals. Either way, I finally had the opportunity I had always wanted, to play Division I baseball. I chose the University of Iowa in early June of my senior summer. I can still remember the day I committed like it was yesterday.

Once on the Iowa campus, my patience was tested again. I had to wait my turn to get on the field. Hitting .083 as a freshman didn't help and it wasn't what I would call a hot start. I didn't get a lot of at bats, and I actually found myself pitching more than playing in the field my first year. After the season, I looked myself in the mirror and realized that there was a lot of room for me to improve. I obviously had a lot that I needed to work on. I spent the next summer back home playing in a summer league trying to figure out what went wrong my freshman year. I spent hours and hours in the cage working on my swing. As much as I wanted immediate results, I knew I wasn't going to get them. I spent the summer focusing on the process of getting better and the hard work and right mind set paid off. I showed up on campus in August, not only as a sophomore, but also as a completely different player.

In my second year at Iowa I worked with a mental conditioning coach by the name of Brian Cain. Working with Brian changed my life. I spent a weekend listening and learning from him, a weekend that that ultimately sparked my interest in Sports Psychology and the mental game. I specifically remember his talk about car headlights and 200 feet at a time. His analogy was that if you drove a car from New York City to Los Angeles and left in the middle of the night, you wouldn't be able to see all the way to your destination. All you could see was the 200 feet right in front of you that your headlights allowed you to. His message was that if you focused on the 200 feet right in front of you, and then after that you focused on the next 200 feet in front of you and so on, you would ultimately reach your destination, and in this case, end up in LA. When traveling, you don't get to your destination focusing on the big picture or thousands of miles in front of you. You get to your destination by taking it 200 feet at a time.

In other words, Brian taught me not to worry so much about the future and where I wanted to go or what I wanted to do. Instead, he taught me to take things one day at a time. If I took care of business today, and then the next day after that, and then the next day after that, I would end up exactly where I wanted to be. He taught me to have patience and take advantage of the time that I had on my hands right now. It's not always about the end result in terms of what you're working for. In school, when you get your grades back at the end of the day, everyone wants to get that "A" when final grades come out. Don't get me wrong, the grade is important, but the end result of the grade isn't quite as important as what you learned and the knowledge you gained along the way. It's the process of getting that final good grade that really counts. Brian's message in his lesson, that it is important to focus on the process, not the result, turned out to be one of the biggest lessons I've learned in my life.

Like college, my path to professional baseball also tested my patience. I broke my arm as a senior at Iowa when I was hit by a pitch in late April in a game against Michigan State. With that one pitch my future became iffy and my goals and dreams seemed to be put on hold. For as long as I could remember I wanted to get drafted and play pro ball. Now, I wasn't sure if that was going to happen. When the draft finally rolled around, I was medically cleared, but anyone who has ever been immobilized for a few months knows that it takes some time to get the strength and flexibility back that you had before an injury.

In the 26th round of the 2009 MLB Draft I got a call from a scout from the Florida Marlins, now the Miami Marlins. He told me that they wanted to take a second baseman in the next round and that I was one they liked. He then asked how my arm was. I felt it was best to be honest and I told him exactly what was up, I was cleared but it would take a few weeks to get back into baseball shape. I hadn't gotten my hopes up that I would be drafted as a result of the injury, but this call had my hopes skyrocketing. As the 27th round came I watched closely on my computer in Iowa City with some former college teammates of mine as the Marlins selected on pick 818 a second baseman from Pepperdine. I got a phone call back from the

Marlins a few rounds later saying they were worried about my arm being healthy and that's why they didn't take me. As a result, I wasn't drafted by the Marlins, or any other team in the 2009 MLB draft.

I spent the next few weeks rehabbing my arm in Iowa City with my athletic trainer, Natalie Bumpass, all while sitting by my phone waiting for it to ring in hopes that someone wanted to offer me a free agent contract. Not only did the time in the training room test my patience, but it also tested Natalie's as well. I had to have patience and trust the rehab process. I also had to realize it was going to take some time before I was back to full strength. I couldn't just snap my fingers and be healed like I would have liked. It was hard for me to do, but with Natalie's help my arm gradually got better and back into the shape I needed for baseball.

During my rehab I had conversations with the Texas Rangers and the Chicago Cubs, but nothing came of it. After about two weeks of waiting I called my college hitting coach, Ryan Brownlee, and he told me I needed to go and find a place to play. He said I needed to show everyone I was healthy, and I agreed. My only option at the time was independent ball, and to be honest I really didn't want to go that route. Yes in independent ball I would get paid to play, but these teams weren't affiliated with a Major League organization. However, it is possible to be signed by an affiliated team out of an independent league. It seemed like my best option at the time, but more importantly, it was my only option.

I have had many friends play in independent leagues and there's nothing wrong with these teams or leagues, but I had it stuck in my mind that I never wanted to go play independent ball. I had tried being patient and letting things work themselves out, but like I said, this was my only remaining option. I had always wanted to sign with a Major League team, so I made the only logical choice I had. I picked up the phone and made a few phone calls. Fortunately enough for me, the Sioux City Explorers of the American Association needed a guy and offered me a contract at the end of June.

I played with the Explorers for 8 games, making trips to Lincoln, Nebraska, Wichita, Kansas, and a few home games in Sioux City, Iowa. I played decent and hit well while mostly playing the middle infield. To this day, I'll never forget that Friday morning in Sioux City when my phone rang. Steve Abney, a scout with the Cleveland Indians was on the other line. He told me the Indians needed a guy and that he had heard good things about me. All of my patience had finally paid off, and I was offered a contract by the Cleveland Indians. On July 7th, 2009, in Ohio my dream was official; I had signed a professional contract with an affiliated organization.

I am a firm believer that things happen for a reason, in one way or another. I feel that the problems and struggles I have encountered in my baseball career have only shown me how to really love, respect, and appreciate the game as I should. It has also helped me grow as a person. Anyone who has ever been hurt will tell you they would do just about anything to get back out on the field. For me, it took an injury to really show me how much this game meant to me. If it wasn't for the patience that I had learned through the tough times and trials of my career, I wouldn't be who I am today or be anywhere close to where I am at right now in my baseball career.

If I hadn't gone through the trials, experienced the hardships, and had my patience tested over and over again, like I've said before, I wouldn't be the person I am today. You see, the process of my college experience and the process of getting into pro ball have ingrained in me many values and life lessons that I would have otherwise never learned. Making it to a Division I athletic program or being a professional athlete isn't what defines me as a person. The end result of wherever my playing career takes me isn't what defines me as a person. At the end of the day what defines me are the many lessons that I have learned through the process of trying to get where I've wanted to go in life. It wasn't the outcome that changed me as a person; it was the life lessons along the way.

Patience not only has helped me in my life, but it can do the same in yours. I am sure if you looked back on your past experiences you would find many times when your patience has been tested. My message to you would be that if you have a dream or you have a goal, go out and get it. If something stands in your way, have the patience to find a way around or through whatever is standing in your way. We live in a "right now" world. Everyone wants to have things done as soon as possible. The thing with that is "right now" isn't always possible, but if you focus on the process, the small things, and take it step by step, eventually, with patience of course, you will end up exactly where you want to be.

Anything is possible in school, in athletics, and in the working world. If you work hard, have the right mind set and a little bit of patience, you can go a long way in life. You might have to do a few things you don't want to, you might have to wait longer than you'd like, you might have to take a few unusual routes to get where you want to go, but if you focus on taking care of business one step at a time and have the patience to allow things to happen, you will end up right where you want to be.

This 2012 season had tested my patience. As I said earlier, I bounced around from team to team and experienced bouts of success separated by bouts of struggle. During those times, I tried not to get too high or too low. Being hard on yourself during a 140 game season will take its toll on you. When I struggled I just had to have patience and believe in myself that I would be able to turn things around. Just like those instances earlier in my career, I had to have patience to make it through this specific game on this night. I also had to make sure I focused on the process even though, as I've mentioned, sometimes it's hard to do.

Once I was back in the dugout for the bottom half of the first, I didn't have a lot of time to relax as I was up second for us this inning. I grabbed my bat and helmet and made my way to the on deck circle to get loose. As I left the dugout a few fans who I usually make small talk with before my first at bat asked if I was excited to play every position. One little kid even asked if I was really going to pitch. I assured them I was ready for the challenge and appreciated them showing their support.

Tonight we were facing Miguel Celestino from Salem. He was a tall righty with a good fastball. Tony Wolters was the lead-off guy for us. Tony was a top prospect in our organization as a middle infielder. He was a good defender and hit from the left side of the plate. He was a high school draft guy with a bright future ahead of him. Celestino didn't start off great and Tony walked on four consecutive pitches. As I made my way to the plate, I got a pretty loud welcome as I was announced. It was a cool feeling having the crowd into the game, but despite that, I had to focus on the task at hand. Since Tony walked on four straight pitches, I knew I had to see a few pitches before I took the bat off my shoulder.

I took the first pitch for a ball, and the second for a called strike. I barely got a piece of the third pitch I saw and fouled it off. I took a step out of the box to refocus, took a deep breath, and then got back in the box. I stood in with a one ball and two strike count, got a good pitch to hit, and laced it into left field just out of the reach of Salem's shortstop James Kang's glove. As I rounded first I let out a huge sigh of relief. Nothing gets rid of the nerves and jitters of a game quite like your first chance at some action, whether it's in the field or at the plate. I also got that first knock out of the way, which as any baseball player knows, is huge in your first at bat. With the single, I could also cross off one of three things on my to do list for the night, a base hit.

With runners on first and second and no outs, our three hole hitter, Giovanny Urshela, hit a ground ball to Salem's third baseman Michael Almanzar, who flipped it to Sean Coyle at second for the force out and the first out of the inning. I was out on the play, but we still had base runners and a chance to score. As I got back to the dugout I was finally able to catch my breath for the first time since the start of the game. After the first pitch everything had happened so quickly up to this point. It's kind of like being in the zone, as you don't really know what's going on until you have a second to stop and think about it. I wanted to make sure I slowed the game down because I wanted to enjoy every second of it.

After catching my breath, I made my way over to the specially made lineup card we were using that outlined everyone's position for each inning of the entire game. Not only would I be playing multiple positions, but others would as well. Edwin, our manager, was convinced that someone would screw up the whole thing if he didn't lay it all out on paper. Looking back, he was probably right. I found my name and made sure I knew the order of the positions I would be playing tonight: right field, center field, left field, first base, second base, shortstop, third base, catcher, and finally pitcher. After I repeated it to myself a few times, I took a deep breath and took a seat on the bench to watch the rest of the inning.

With runners on the corners, Ronny Rodriguez lined into a double play to end our scoring threat. The first inning was over. Neither team scored and the scoreboard showed zeros in the run column after one inning of play. After a quick drink of Gatorade I got up off the bench and tried to gather myself. With all of the emotions I felt, I simply reminded myself to stay relaxed, stay in the present moment, try not to do too much, and go out there and have fun. I then grabbed my hat and glove and made my way out to the field and my next position.

Chapter 2
Perspective

"Is the glass half empty, or is it half full?"

"A pessimist sees the difficulty in every opportunity; an optimist sees the opportunity in every difficulty."
- Winston Churchill

Growing up I always envisioned playing one of three positions in my backyard. I was always the shortstop, the pitcher, or the centerfielder. As a kid, those were always the main guys and stars you would see on TV. You turn on Sportscenter and you would see shortstops like Derek Jeter, centerfielders like Ken Griffey Jr. and pitchers like Greg Maddux. Those were the kind of guys I always wanted to be. I was fortunate enough growing up to be able to pitch and play shortstop quite a bit. My first baseball jersey was number thirty-one in honor of Maddux, and if anyone watched me play in high school, college, or on this particular night in Carolina, they would have seen number two on my back, in honor of my favorite player growing up, Derek Jeter.

Center field was the one position I never got much of a chance to play. Sure, I played it when I was growing up, but the older I got, the more I focused on pitching and playing the infield. My freshman year of high school I played occasionally in left field but that was it. In college I never went beyond the infield dirt. It wasn't until professional baseball that I found myself in the outfield on a somewhat regular basis. Before this night, I couldn't tell you the last time I found myself in center field.

As the inning started I was amazed at the change in scenery. From center field you could see everything. I had a clear view of the strike zone, a great view of the pitch, and an entire view of the field. I was able to read the hitter's swing pretty well, get a good jump on the ball, and also be able to anticipate where the ball would be hit depending on the location of the pitch. Above all of that, on this night, I also had a spectacular view of a pretty packed Five County Stadium.

Anyone who has ever switched positions on the baseball field knows the different perceptions of the game that each position portrays. For me, the biggest change growing up was switching from my natural position of shortstop to the other side of the diamond and second base. It was such a different perspective from the left side to the right side of the infield. Neither of those even compared to center field for me. The view of the stadium, seeing the entire infield walk their way into a ready position and pre-pitch setup before each pitch, or even hearing the echoes of the voices of my teammates off of the center field wall. It put baseball into a whole new perspective for me.

The other thing that's different about the outfield is how boring it is, at least for me. Playing the middle infield allows you to pretty much be involved on every pitch, whether it's backing up the pitcher on throws back from the catcher or throwing the ball around the infield after a strikeout. Being close to the action allows you to feel more engaged and with your close proximity to the hitter you must be ready for the ball to be rocketed at you every time the ball leaves the pitchers hand. In the outfield, you're lucky if you have a ball hit to you once or twice a game, let alone in one inning.

The top half of the second inning allowed me to get the ball while it was in play for the first time. I moved over to center field and Cid moved from center over to right field. The first hitter of the inning for Salem, Drew Hedman, struck out swinging. Salem's second baseman, Sean Coyle, was then hit by a pitch. Our pitcher, Jordan Cooper, notched his third strikeout of the evening on the next hitter, David Renfroe. With Coyle on first and two outs, the next hitter, David Chester, singled sharply up the middle to me in center field. Coyle immediately left on contact and made his way safely into third base.

I might have had a play on Coyle and had a chance to throw him out, but instead of trying to do too much, especially in a position I wasn't all that familiar with, I kept the ball of front of me and fired it into second base. With Renfroe's single, there were now runners on the corners with two outs. Coop then took care of business and finished off the inning by getting Jayson Hernandez to pop out to Ronny Rodriguez at shortstop. We kept Salem off the scoreboard again and headed towards the dugout for the bottom of the second inning.

We hadn't had much luck playing Salem during this particular season. It seemed like whenever they played us they crushed everything, and I mean everything. They were an aggressive team and had scored a ton of runs against us, to the tune of eight a couple times, ten, twelve, and even sixteen at different times this season. For us to hold them scoreless early on was a huge boost to our team's confidence heading into the middle of the game.

The different perspective of playing center field on this night struck a chord with me, my career, and my life. Often times in life, the way you think and how you perceive things are vital to your success or your failures. It's crazy how you can take one event or one object and two different people can perceive that object or event differently. The easiest example of this would be the old glass of water question. If there is a glass sitting in front of you, and it is filled up halfway with water, is it half full or half empty? You always hear people say the pessimist says it's half empty, but the optimist says it's half full. The cool thing about all of that is your perception of that event is solely based on how you think.

As I mentioned before, my sophomore year at the University of Iowa, and to this day, I have had the pleasure of working with Brian Cain. If you have ever met him or worked with him in any fashion, you know he's an extremely motivational person. He'll make you feel like you can run through a brick wall and eat fire, literally (been there, done that). The thing I love about him and what he teaches is that he challenges the way you think. Brian brought to my attention one of the best examples of perception I have ever seen. Have you ever seen the FedEx logo, the one on all of the delivery trucks driving around? I am sure you have, probably many times. Even though you have seen it many times have you ever noticed the arrow in the empty space between the E and the X at the end of the logo? If not, check out the logo below and find the arrow.

Pretty cool and crazy isn't it? The cool thing about it is that the arrow has always been there, it just took a change of perception, a change of thinking, to see it. There are a lot of different perception-

FedEx service marks used by permission.

changing images out there. You can search online for different ones. Search for "old man or the young lady", "two faces or a vase", and also the "3D cube". If you look at those pictures one way, you see the first in the set, the old man, the two faces, or a cube in one direction. If you change your perception and how you look at the picture, you'll see a young lady, a vase, and a cube in a different direction. The picture itself never changes, but how you look at it does and that makes all the difference.

This lesson not only works on really cool pictures, but it works in athletics and life. If you change the way you look at something or change the way you think about something, you open up a whole new world, and sometimes a whole new set of opportunities. A lot of times people perceive their problems as impossible to overcome. What people don't realize is that if you change the way you look at a problem and change the way you think about a problem, many times you find ways around or through that problem, or you may even find that it's not even a problem at all.

Another exercise that demonstrates a change in perception involves a two by four board. This particular demonstration makes sense of how you can look at a task, and even though the task is the same, the way you perceive it is drastically different. If you lay a two by four board on the ground and have someone walk across it, they'll tell you it's relatively easy to do. Now let's say you raise the board off the ground and use it to make a walkway that connects two tables roughly four or five feet off the ground. If that same person again performed the task they would tell you that this one was harder than the previous attempt.

The question this exercise raises is how is it possible the task gets harder when the task stays the same – walking across the board. No matter how high off the ground or how low to the ground the board is, the task of walking across it is always the same. The only thing that changes is your perception of the task. The perceived danger of falling makes the second task seem harder, even though it is the same task as the board being on the floor.

This happens all the time in athletics. People perceive things and sometimes make them harder than they really are. If you're a pitcher, it shouldn't matter who the batter is that you're facing. It doesn't matter if it's your mom or dad or Josh Hamilton or Miguel Cabrera standing in the box. The task of making quality pitches, playing pitch to pitch, and battling your rear end off doesn't change. If you're a hitter it doesn't matter who is on the mound. Your task of having a good approach, getting a good pitch to hit, and timing it up doesn't change. Too often we let other people dictate our perception of an event instead of seeing the event or task as what it really is.

As a professional athlete whose season runs March through September, I have to work to make money in the off season when I'm not playing. As many baseball players do, I give lessons. I enjoy working with kids who have dreams and aspirations and I enjoy helping them along their path to achieve those things. As anyone knows with youth athletics, as well as middle school and high school teams, usually there is a varsity, junior varsity, and freshman team, or an A, B, or C team. Everyone wants to be on that A team, or the varsity team, but, depending on the sport, there are only a few select spots on each team.

One off season I was working with a kid and the topic of changing the way you think and changing your perception came up. He wasn't the greatest athlete, but what impressed me most about this kid was that he had the right mindset and was looking at things with the right perspective. He was going to be an 8th grader in the fall and his coach had asked some guys from the 8th grade team to bump down and play on the 7th grade team. Because his age fit the requirements he was able to do so. Many kids would look at this as a demotion or as a problem. They would think that they aren't good enough, that they'll never make it, or that the coach doesn't know what he is talking about. This particular kid looked at it in a different way. He looked at this as an opportunity to play more games, get more at bats, and become a better baseball player. That's the kind of mindset a winner has, and as a result, he improved tremendously.

Along the same lines, I can find examples of this in my own life. I was never a very big kid and was often told I was too small for this or not strong enough for that. I first tried football in middle school, and I played for both the A team and the B team. I didn't know or realize it at the time, but looking back on it I was able to spend more time on the field, and as a result I learned more and became a much better player. Had I only been on the A team I could only have played 4 quarters. Playing on both teams allowed me to play 6-8 quarters providing me many more opportunities for improvement.

Flash forward to my sophomore year in high school and the same thing happened in basketball. I would start on the JV team, play 2-3 quarters with them, and then suit up for with the varsity squad and play 3-4 quarters more quarters with those guys. That year, I made huge strides as a basketball player. By no means was I a super star, but my junior and senior years I had more success because of the time I spent playing on JV as a sophomore. My ball handling skills improved, my shooting improved, but more importantly my decision-making improved. As hard as you practice, and as much as you try to create game situations in practice, nothing can get you better prepared for a real game than actually playing in real games. Had I only suited varsity and let my ego tell me I was too good for JV, I wouldn't have seen the improvements nor would I have gained the valuable experience I got that season.

Another great example of having the right perspective in athletics is in my hometown of Council Bluffs, Iowa with the Attack Volleyball Club. I've gotten to know Mark Andrews, Jenyi Bergsten, and a little about the club from my time working at Midwest Sporting Goods. The rule with Attack is that no one gets cut after tryouts. Everyone has a team whether it's the A team, B team, or C team of each age group. Mark makes a point to let the girls know that when teams come out, they aren't set in stone and you can move up or move down depending on performance and improvement.

This makes a lot of sense to me when talking about youth sports. Mark has mentioned multiple times that sometimes girls from the C team or D team at ages twelve or thirteen end up being his best players by the time they are sixteen and seventeen. The players that do move up do so not because they looked at not being on the A team as a negative, but rather because they looked at it as a positive. It allowed them to work on their game and get better, rather than sitting on the bench and not playing much with a higher team.

What all of these stories have in common is that these athletes took what most people would call a problem and turned it into an opportunity. They changed their perspective. They saw the white arrow in the FedEx logo when everyone else was too busy looking at the first thing that showed up, the logo and the team or level they were playing at. The ones who saw the arrow took an opportunity to get better instead of having the problem of not being associated with the top team. I'll tell you one thing, when it comes to the game of life, these kinds of kids, the ones who look at those situations as a positive, can be on my team any day.

Athletes that are very successful rarely think negatively. They will take the same everyday problems a normal person would look at and say "why me" to and answer it with "why not me". You will be amazed at how much more enjoyable your experiences are in life when you think positively and have the right perspective. Next time you're in a tough spot, look at whatever is in front of you with a change of perspective, look at it as an opportunity, not as a problem. You don't have to be in the Major Leagues, the NFL, or the NBA to be able to do this. All you need to do to be effective with a change in perspective is to change the way you think and how you see things in your life.

If you happened to make it out to Five Country Stadium on this night or during the 2012 season, in the bottom of the second inning you may have played or experienced a little game called TooleTime Trivia. It's the new modern day version of trivia where I was always an option as one of the possible four answers to a Trivia Question, even if it made absolutely no sense. It was always a multiple choice question and it was always played up on the video board. I, of course, along with a few loyal fans, always thought I was the correct answer.

One of my favorite TooleTime Trivia questions of the season was along the lines of which player was born in such and such country, the country being one of either the Dominican Republic, Puerto Rico, Columbia, or Venezuela. Among the possible answers were guys like Ronny Rodriguez, Jesus Aguilar, Delvi Cid, Giovanny Urshela, Jose Flores, Francisco Jimenez, Danny Salazar and of course Justin Toole. TooleTime Trivia was always fun and always gave me something to look forward to and laugh at in between innings. My teammates and the fans enjoyed it as well.

On this particular night, the trivia question was this: Mudcats super-utility man Justin Toole earned which honor during the 2011 season? The options for answers were: A, Carolina League All Star. B, Indians Hitter of the Week. C, Carolina League Player of the Week. Or D, Greatest Tweeter of All Time. The answer was A, as I was a Carolina League All Star the year before. (But to this day I will argue that both A and D were correct.)

In the bottom of the second inning we pushed across our first two runs of the game. Tyler Cannon led off hitting a ball hard, only it was right at the shortstop Kang for the first out of the inning. Todd Hankins was then hit by a pitch and quickly stole second base. As he slid into second the catcher's throw got away from the middle infielders, and he easily scooted over to third. Hankins' heads-up base running had him 90 feet closer to scoring the first run of the game. With Hankins on third and one out, Dwight Childs struck out swinging. Marcus Bradley then walked to put runners on the corners for Delvi Cid. Cid got a good pitch to hit and crushed a ball into center field over Brandon Jacobs head for a double. As the ball reached the wall Hankins and Bradley both raced home and scored the first two runs of the game. With Cid on second, Tony Wolters then grounded out to second baseman Sean Coyle to end the inning.

I think in this game it was important to take an early lead. With Salem having smacked us in the mouth a few times earlier in the season, it was important to change the perception that they weren't going to do that again. We had lost to them the night before 8-2, and so to get the momentum in our dugout early on was huge. Often, when teams roll into a game thinking they will win and find themselves behind early, they can't quite recover. Hopefully, tonight would be one of those times for Salem.

The other cool thing about the night was that the crowd was really into the game. I don't know if it was the anticipation of me playing all the positions or the good Saturday night Yuengling beer deals (I'd say probably the beer deals). All I know is that it's really fun to play in front of fans that are into the game. It helped not only that we had jumped out with a few runs early, but also that our pitcher Jordan Cooper was dealing. He had been lights out for us the past few weeks and he carried that momentum right into tonight. I couldn't wait to hopefully close the door on the mound in the ninth inning for a Mudcats victory.

Chapter 3

Expensive and Inexpensive Experience

"Experience is what you get when you didn't get what you wanted. And experience is often the most valuable thing you have to offer."
— Randy Pausch

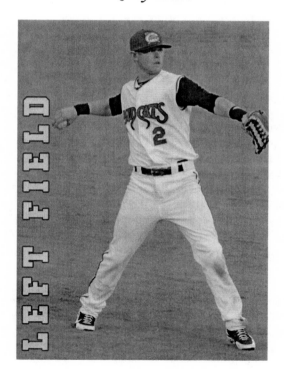

The top of the third inning finished my tour of the outfield. It was also my last chance to catch a ball in the outfield as the two previous innings yielded nothing in the defensive box score. Having played left field a little bit prior to tonight, this was easily my most comfortable position beyond the dirt of the infield. Our bullpen sits down the left field line and it is routine for one of the pitchers to warm up the leftfielder. I always enjoy playing left field because down the left field line at Five County Stadium sits some of the best (in terms of loud and vocal) fans we have. Tonight's game was no different. The crowd was loud and into the game. While you're warming up, numerous kids and a few adults scream at you wanting baseballs. They tell you you're their favorite player and they love you and on and on. My teammates and I call this the boy band treatment, and nothing beat the Five County Stadium boy band treatment on this night.

If you've ever played professional baseball or even college baseball, one of the many things you will hear over and over every day is "can I have a ball". No matter what day of the week, no matter what city or park you're in, you will always have people asking you for a ball. I am here to set the record straight: if a baseball player doesn't give you a ball when you ask for one, it isn't that he's a mean guy. It only means that you are the 123,098,839,283rd person to ask for one that day and there are only so many baseballs to go around. I will give you a hint (some inexpensive experience) to better your chances of getting a ball. I'm not saying it will work, but it always helps to refer to the player by their first name. If you repeatedly yell, "Hey number 12 can I have a ball", chances are he won't give you one or even acknowledge you for that matter. However, if you call out to a player using their first name you just might get their attention and quite possibly get a ball.

As I moved over to left field from center field, Delvi Cid moved back to center field from right field, and Marcus Bradley then moved from left field over to right field. Each inning it seemed like there were more and more position changes. Now you're starting to get the picture as to why Edwin made a full lineup card detailing everyone's position from inning to inning. Lucas LeBlanc led off the inning for Salem and popped out to Ronny Rodriguez at shortstop. James Kang then hit the ball hard to center field for a double. With Kang in scoring position and one out, the next batter, Michael Almanzar, hit a fly ball right to Bradley in right field for out number two of the inning. The last batter of the inning, Brandon Jacobs followed up as yet another Jordan Cooper strikeout victim.

We had held Salem scoreless for three innings in large part to the great pitching of Jordan Cooper. Coop's not a guy who is going to blow you away with anything by putting up huge numbers on the radar gun, but what he is good at is hitting his spots and knowing how to pitch. He's not the kind of guy who will beat himself and he knows how to compete on the mound. This night it looked like he was on his "A" game, which meant a big headache for the Salem hitters. From a defensive perspective it's always nice to have a guy like Coop on the mound. He pitches with pace and gets after hitters. Playing defense for that kind of pitcher always allows you to better stay in the flow of the game, and as a result, the defense usually makes plays behind their pitcher. This night was proving to be no different.

Playing left field got me to thinking back on how I originally found myself playing this position. Playing left field in professional baseball happened as the result of an injury to one of my teammates. In sports, a lot of opportunities open up as a result of injuries. You always see someone get hurt and then a guy steps in with a chance to play and never looks back. A few years earlier in Kinston, a teammate of mine, Abner Abreu, hurt his arm throwing a ball during pre-game infield and outfield. It wasn't anything serious but it was enough to keep him out of the lineup. We didn't have many options of guys to take his spot so I volunteered to do so to our manager, Aaron Holbert. I told him I could play left field if he needed and sure enough I found myself starting in left field that evening.

I had never really played much outfield growing up, but I was confident I could play the position and play the position well. One thing I learned growing up was the difference between expensive experience and inexpensive experience. I learned that in sports you can learn a lot just through watching what other people do (inexpensive experience) as well as learning through your own mistakes and experiences (expensive experience). I had volunteered to play a position I wasn't familiar with because I had the confidence to play there as a result of inexpensive experience.

I was fortunate enough to grow up in a baseball family. My dad was a good high school player with aspirations of playing in college and professionally until knee injuries slowed him down. My mom was also a great athlete, playing two college sports, one of which was softball. My sister was a good athlete growing up as she was involved in dance, basketball, and of course softball. My brother was a standout athlete in football, basketball, track and baseball. Our family was always on the run to an athletic event or dance event of some sort when I was growing up. I was very lucky being born into a family like this and was able to learn a lot growing up as a result of that.

My dad's love for baseball carried over into a coaching career. He's been a high school baseball coach ever since I was born, winning an Iowa State Championship and being named Iowa Coach of the year in 1993. Just a few years ago, in 2011, he was named National High School Coach of the Year for his contributions to the sport. He has taken numerous teams to state tournaments, a few of which I participated on, and has been inducted into the Iowa High School Baseball Coaches Association Hall of Fame. He's won close to 800 games over a 30 year career. Not bad for a coach, and not a bad guy to learn the game of baseball from.

The benefit of being a coach's kid is that you can always show up to practice and watch or even participate. For as long as I can remember I was always trying to find my way into a hitting station or a fielding station to try and hang with the high school kids at my dad's practices. It didn't matter how old I was, I was always out there, even at the age of 9 and 10. Some of my dad's old players who are grown up now still tell me to this day how I would show up and play catch with kids much older than me like it was nothing. They'd tell me I would ask them if that's all they've got when I played catch with them or tell them I could hit and field better than they could. (People now will tell you things haven't changed much!) I guess you can say I was just born with confidence and maybe, at times, a big mouth too.

Watching many games growing up, either as the bat boy, sitting in the stands, or watching on TV, I always tried to pay attention to what was going on out on the field. Little did I know, I was giving myself priceless inexpensive experience. I was the kid who would watch a shortstop make a great play and go home and try to duplicate it the next day. I would see a player jack a home run and the next day at home I would try and do the same. The best way to learn something is to immerse yourself in it. I immersed myself into the game of baseball growing up and as a result I learned a lot about how to play the game.

When I volunteered to play left field that day in Kinston, it was because I had watched many guys play left field and other outfield positions throughout my life. I figured learning from others was the best route to go, and I had done a lot of that by watching my dad's teams growing up. I also tried to pick the brain of the other outfielders on the team before the game. I had a quick little run through with my manager and coaches to make sure I was fully capable of playing out there before the game started. After holding my own and showing the coaches I was actually capable of playing out there, I was given the green light to go. I was able to play out there in left field not because I had practiced it over and over, but rather because I paid attention and learned from my teammates who regularly played out there.

Nothing quite replaces the knowledge of expensive experience or actually going through something yourself, but inexpensive experience can carry you a long way. I found left field to have its tough times, but it was pretty much as I had imagined. A few things are different in the outfield in comparison to the infield. You don't have to play as low to the ground because you have more time to react to the ball when it's hit to you. You have to know the nooks and crannies of the outfield wall, like how the ball bounces off different parts of the wall in order to field the ball and get it back into the infield as quickly as possible. You also have to focus in on the game with the fans in the outfield bleachers harassing you. Maybe the worst thing about the outfield is you also get more bug bites because you're standing in the grass rather than the dirt. As I mentioned before, I also find it to be extremely boring compared to the infield. I'll always consider myself an infielder, but I do enjoy playing out there in the outfield occasionally.

Playing baseball and other sports for as long as I can remember has allowed me many opportunities to learn from inexpensive experience and watching others. I have learned from fellow teammates and coaches, opposing players and coaches, as well as from being a spectator. I always try to make a habit of talking to people who have gotten to the places I want to get to and picked their brain or asked for advice. If you're a high school player who wants to play in college, find a college kid who is doing what you want to do and ask him questions that can help you get to the next level. If you're a high school coach looking for drills or new knowledge, don't be afraid to ask local college coaches or other high school coaches what they do. Most kids and coaches would gladly spend a little bit of time talking to you. That's one of the easiest and best ways to gain inexpensive experience.

Playing in the Indians Organization I have had the pleasure of working with and talking with some pretty knowledgeable baseball people, managers, big league players, minor league players, and front office staff. Being a utility guy, I don't play every day all the time, so I take advantage of watching the game and learning from my teammates when I'm not in the lineup. I have also had the opportunity to suit up and be around Cleveland's Major League spring training camp and I have gained a great wealth of knowledge just by watching how people conduct themselves and how they play the game. As an athlete or coach you can do the same thing in your area with the resources around you. It might not be in a Major League setting, but you can still learn a lot from watching successful people in your area.

If you look at the most successful people in life, many of them are where they are because they have learned from their mistakes. Take Michael Jordan's great quote as an example, "I've missed more than 9,000 shots in my career. I've lost almost 300 games. 26 times, I've been trusted to take the game winning shot and missed. I've failed over and over and over again in my life. And that is why I succeed." What Jordan is trying to say is that the reason he succeeds is because of the expensive experience he has developed in his life. He hasn't always been perfect. He has made mistakes, he has missed shots, he has lost games, but that hasn't kept him from learning from those situations which in turn has made him a better basketball player.

Baseball is a game of failure. Anyone who plays or knows the sport knows that if you repeatedly go 4-10 you're an All-American in college and if you repeatedly go 3-10 in the Major Leagues you'll be in the Hall of Fame. That means that you will fail much more than you succeed and despite that, you will still be considered successful. The sooner you accept the fact that you will make mistakes and you're not perfect, the sooner you can start to learn from your mistakes. Baseball and many athletic sports are games of adjustments. The best players are the ones who learn from past experiences and continue to get better; they use failures as teaching points. They don't use failure negatively; instead they use it positively, to help them get better.

My freshman year of high school, my baseball team was rated the number one team in 4A in the state of Iowa heading into the state tournament. The number two team at state, Marshalltown, would be our second round opponent if we won, a team that we had beaten 10-0 in six innings earlier in the season. Everyone was pretty pumped up as we were a legitimate State Title contender, if not the favorite. As a result, we took our first round opponent, Des Moines Roosevelt, lightly. We played terribly and lost the game by a run. I fielded a ground ball late in the game and overthrew first base which allowed what would end up being the winning run to reach base. The team we beat earlier in the year, Marshalltown, ended up winning the title that year.

I learned a very important piece of expensive experience at the State Tournament that day. I learned to not ever look past an opponent. It's not the best team that wins, it's the team that plays the best, and on that particular day, Des Moines Roosevelt played better than we did even though we were the more talented team. As a result, Roosevelt, as they deserved to, won the game and we packed our bags and headed home.

In college I found myself on the other side of a couple similar situations. I remember winning two games against Vanderbilt and Nebraska. At the time they were both ranked as top 10 teams in the nation. On those particular days we played fundamental baseball and played better than both of those schools even though they were vastly more talented than we were. As a result we beat both of them. To me it only drove home the fact that you can't overlook teams and that you have to come ready to play every single day. It's always the team that plays the best that wins, it's not necessarily the most talented team that does.

If there is just one piece of inexpensive experience you take away from this book, I hope it would be this: It's not the best team that wins, it's the team that plays the best, and it's not always the best player that has a great game, but rather the player who plays the best. The beauty about sports is that anyone can beat anyone on any given day. That is why you play the game. It doesn't matter who you are playing, what the front of their jersey says, or what the name on the back says. All that matters is the group of guys who plays together and plays the best is going to be the group who wins the game. Upsets happen all the time, that's what makes sports so awesome. Don't ever go into a game and think that you can't win. If you think you can't win you're done before the game even started.

Back to the game. Heading into the bottom of the third inning, we were on the right side of the game thus far. I was due to leadoff the inning against Celestino, who was still out on the mound. Having singled in my first at bat, I had a lot of confidence heading to the plate. I got a good pitch to hit but got under it just a little. The result was a routine fly out to Jacobs in center field. I might have been trying to do a little too much with the pitch, but, ultimately, I was the first out of the inning. That brought Giovanny Urshela up to the plate. Gio was our usual 3rd baseman but he got the start as the DH in this game. He was a pretty good hitter and when he got a good pitch to hit he would let it fly. On the first pitch Gio saw from Celestino, he did just that. He hammered the pitch to right field for a solo home run.

As our team congratulated him in the dugout, Gio had that usual smile that you always see on his face. He was a young kid from Columbia who it seemed always had a smile on his face, and I mean always. You could never tell if he had a bad game or a great game. He was just always happy. He always had the same demeanor no matter what his results of the game were. When you asked him why he's like that, he would just shrug his shoulder and say, "I don't know, just be happy". Not only was he happy and smiling, but his moon-shot had everyone else happy as well. With one swing of the bat Gio had stretched our lead to three runs.

Ronny Rodriguez was up next and took some healthy hacks at a few pitches. Ronny can be a little bit of a free swinger at times and as a result Celestino struck him out swinging. That brought up Tyler Cannon. Tyler didn't like any of the pitches he saw and with two outs, he walked. With Tyler on first, Todd Hankins came to the plate. Todd got a great pitch to hit and he hit it hard. The only problem was that he hit it right at the second baseman. Coyle caught the ball easily for the last out of the inning.

Still, we were able to tack another run on the board, which was huge. You'll always hear coaches say to keep pouring the runs on after you score early. Too often teams will put a few runs up in the first few innings and then shut it down only to allow the other team back in the game. As it looked right now, that didn't appear to be the case for us. Having had it handed to us by Salem a few times this year, we knew we had to score as many runs as possible. Hopefully we could continue to do that the rest of the game.

As the inning ended, I grabbed my hat and glove and almost started out to the field when I realized I needed a different glove than the one I had been using previously. Having played outfield the previous three innings, I was holding on to my outfield glove about to run out to first base with it. Luckily I noticed in time and I was able to make the quick switch. With the proper gear in hand, I then made my way out to first base. I definitely enjoyed the run to first base much better than the run to left field the inning before. Playing the first couple innings in the grass was a little foreign to me and I was definitely excited to be back on the infield dirt again.

Chapter 4
Take Advantage of Your Opportunities

"Twenty years from now you will be more disappointed by the things that you didn't do than by the ones you did do." – Mark Twain

"It is not often that a man can make opportunities for himself. But he can put himself in such shape that when or if the opportunities come he is ready." – Theodore Roosevelt

I had survived the first three innings. Nothing too exciting had happened so far other than our team putting three runs up on the scoreboard. I did get a hit early on, but defensively I had yet to make any plays aside from fielding a base hit up the middle in center field. The single did take care of one of my three goals for the night and my other two goals were still intact. I hadn't made an error thus far in the game and a team victory was a legit possibility, but I couldn't cross those two goals off quite yet.

The top of the 4th inning at Five County Stadium starts off with a race around the bases between a lucky young child and our mascot Muddy the Mudcat. I don't know what Muddy's deal is, but he never seems to cross the finish line first. I don't think anyone was surprised when this night turned out much like the previous races this season. Mini Muddy, a miniature sized Muddy mascot or someone in the infield always seemed to get in Muddy's way. Tonight I took the opportunity to give Muddy's competition a few extra seconds to build a lead. It worked like a charm and like always, Muddy lost yet again.

As I began to roll some ground balls to my fellow infielders to begin the 4th inning, I took a glance around to see the infield crew I was working with. Tyler Cannon, who had been playing first base up until this inning, was over at third base. Tony Wolters was at second base. To round it out, Ronny Rodriguez was over at shortstop. This particular infield group was familiar with each other and comfortable working together. I found myself playing first base quite a few times this year, and usually when I did Tyler was over at third base. Ronny and Tony often switched every so many games up the middle so they were both used to playing shortstop and second base. All of us were not only familiar with the positions we were playing, but we were also familiar with the faces at each position.

Playing the infield brings you closer to the action. You're closer to home plate, closer to the stands, closer to umpires and closer to the opposing team. Playing first base allows you the chance to talk with the first base umpire, the first base coach, and also any opposing base runners that reach base. I'm not a guy who goes out of my way to try and make small talk with the opposing team, but I will say a few words if the time presents itself.

The first base umpire for tonight's game was Rich Gonzalez. You have to understand that in the Carolina League there are only eight teams, which means four games a night. Therefore, you see the same umpire crews quite a few times throughout the season. Rich and I had our share of ups and downs (typical baseball player/coach and umpire relationship) throughout the season, but I'll be the first to admit that umpiring is a tough job. If you do a great job of umpiring no one says a word to you. On the flip side, if you don't do a very good job of umpiring, everyone has something to say to you. We made typical small talk and like always I lobbied for him to help me out if I hit a ball and the play at first was a close one. I told him I needed a few hits to help boost my average to finish the season strong. Like most umpires I talked to about these issues, he looked right back at me with a smile and told me that wasn't going to happen.

The first batter of the fourth inning was Drew Hedman. He battled himself to a 2-2 count. He then took the next pitch from Jordan Cooper and smacked it right back up the middle for a leadoff single. With Hedman on first, the next batter, Sean Coyle, flew out to center field. That was quickly followed up by outs number two and three on pop ups. David Renfroe hit a pop up to Wolters at second base and David Chester hit one to Ronny at shortstop. Hedman did manage to steal second in between the infield fly outs, but Coop shut the door on the fourth inning. After giving up that leadoff hit he got us back in the dugout after a relatively quick inning.

The difference in the game thus far was really the fact that we had taken advantage of our opportunities with runners in scoring position while Salem hadn't. A couple times they had guys on second and third, but weren't able to push them across. The reason they weren't able to score was largely due to some quality pitching and strong defensive plays in the field. My team, on the other hand, took advantage of a big Delvi Cid double in the second inning to push two across, and then Gio took advantage of a good pitch to tack on another run on his solo home run. Just two swings were really the difference in the game.

One of my favorite sayings that I always try to tell and teach people I speak to or work with is to take advantage of your opportunities. Too often in life, people look for these huge opportunities to just fall in their lap. Hardly if ever does that happen. Usually the best opportunities show up disguised as problems, and as I mentioned in chapter two, your perception is key to seeing those problems as opportunities. Every single day you should try and take advantage of an opportunity you are presented with, whether it is a big opportunity or just a small one.

It's crazy to think how I got my start as a first baseman to begin with. The whole reason I started playing first in the Indians system was through an unexpected opportunity. Unfortunately, as with left field, it was due to an injury. A teammate of mine, Jesus Aguilar, was hit by a pitch in the face in extended spring training back in early 2010. He was one of our primary first baseman and as a result of the injury he missed a couple weeks of action. We needed a first baseman and I stepped in and tried to fill the void. I took advantage of an opportunity to learn how to play first and get my feet wet over the course of a couple weeks while Jesus was out with his injury. At the time, I never really thought much of it, but after a few successful games over there, I officially added first base to my repertoire.

That's the thing with opportunities; you never know when they will show up or where they may lead. On a hot sunny afternoon in Arizona I stepped in at first base and never looked back. A few years later, being a successful defensive utility player has kept me a spot and a job in professional baseball and given me an opportunity to play all nine positions in a game. I play first base pretty routinely now, and playing first is a huge part of what I am able to do in order to help the team. It allows for me to keep my teammates fresh and keep their bats in the lineup as a designated hitter without the wear and tear their legs would get by playing out in the field.

To get an opportunity to play professional baseball was something I had dreamed of my whole life. When the opportunity with the Cleveland Indians came about, I was told I would be a back-up middle infielder for our short season rookie team, the Mahoning Valley Scrappers. I was also told that I would have to earn a trip to Spring Training the following year and that nothing was guaranteed. I had signed a multi-year year contract, but like any job, I could be released from that contract at any time. I took it upon myself to prove to the people of the organization that I belonged and deserved a spot. I took advantage of that opportunity and had a decent season split between Mahoning Valley and our other rookie team in the Arizona League. As a result, I was invited back the following year, and then year after that, and then the year after that.

If you look up my professional stats, they won't jump off the page at you. My batting average isn't eye popping; I don't have many home runs, RBI's, or any of those numbers everyone likes to look at, but I do have a pretty solid fielding percentage playing at many different positions. However, none of those statistics are what I can say I am most proud of during my career. Hands down, what I am most proud of is that I have taken advantage of the opportunities I have been given.

I have had the chance to move up and down the Indians Organization and I am proud to tell you I have done well in that role. Whether it's being the guy on the bench ready to pinch run or the starting shortstop for the evening, I have taken full advantage of those opportunities. Sure, I want to be an everyday player, I mean who doesn't, but I can't worry about that. What I can worry about is taking advantage of what I've been given and I'm proud to tell you that I feel I have done a great job of that thus far in my career.

Speaking of taking advantage of an opportunity, ever heard of Wally Pipp? If you're a baseball fan, chances are you have, and if not, here's a little background info on him. Wally was a Major League baseball player in the 1910's and 1920's, most notably for playing for the New York Yankees. One day, in 1925, he showed up with a bad headache and was scratched from the lineup. He was replaced by a young man named Lou Gehrig.

Lou Gehrig stepped in that day and then proceeded to go on and play in the next 2,130 straight games. His record, which was eventually broken by Cal Ripken Jr., earned him the nickname the "Iron Horse". Wally Pipp never got his spot back in the Yankees line up and his career was never really the same from that point forward. Pipp was said to have been quoted on the incident and the headache with this remark, "I took the two most expensive aspirin in history."

Gehrig did what most successful people in the world do, he took advantage of an opportunity. The opportunity, a small one, the chance to fill in for Pipp for the afternoon, turned into a record breaking 2,130 consecutive games played streak. Gehrig is a great example of someone who took a small opportunity and literally turned it into history. He was famously quoted in his speech at Yankee Stadium as saying, "Yet today, I consider myself the luckiest man on the face of the Earth." Gehrig is a great example of luck as it is sometimes stated that luck happens when preparation meets opportunity. He was prepared and took advantage of his start on that one afternoon. Everyone can learn from this story, whether it's filling in and temporarily taking someone's spot or having someone fill your void for awhile. As Gehrig showed, temporary can easily change into permanent.

I am sure at some point you've asked someone to take your spot for something or to fill in for you for awhile, whether it's on the sports field or in the working world. Or the opposite might be true, where you've been asked to take over for someone else. Don't think because you are "filling in" for someone that you can't make that your permanent spot or that because someone is "filling in" for you, you will automatically be back in that spot tomorrow. Keep Lou Gehrig in the back of your mind when you come to a situation like this. Like I said before, temporary can easily be changed to permanent if you take advantage of the opportunity in front of you.

After my sophomore year at the University of Iowa I headed up north to Wisconsin for the summer. I was set to play in the Northwoods League, a prestigious collegiate summer league with teams in Minnesota, Wisconsin, Iowa, Michigan, and Canada. Upon going there, I had to sign a contract for the summer to play for the La Crosse Loggers. The contract that I had signed was only for ten days, making me a temporary player. Summer leagues often sign players to temporary contracts to fill the void of players who are playing in the NCAA Tournament and possibly the College World Series if their college teams make it that far. You can sign up to two ten day contracts, if I remember right, before you are either allowed to sign a full contract or you are sent home.

I turned my ten day contract into two wonderful summers in La Crosse. My host family for all of that time, Mike and Joyce Diveley, had only planned on me staying for a few weeks. Usually ten day contract guys don't stick around long, but I guess you could say they just couldn't get rid of me. I owe them a huge thank you for putting up with me that whole time. I couldn't have asked for a better family to stay with and I thoroughly enjoyed the entire experience both as a player and as a person.

My first season I worked my way into the lineup everyday as a second baseman, winning the team's defensive player of the year award that was given away at the end of the season. I returned the following summer and played a few different spots on the infield. I didn't allow the term "temporary" ever to cross my mind when I signed that ten day contract. I had it stuck in my mind that once I was there, I was there to stay. I took advantage of the opportunity of having a summer contract and as a result learned a lot and grew as a baseball player. Throughout my whole career, to this day, some of my best memories of baseball came from those summers I spent in La Crosse.

Although you want to take advantage of your opportunities, you never want to take advantage of the people you meet on your life journey while trying to achieve your dreams. My college coach Ryan Brownlee used to always tell me, "You see the same people on the way up as you do on the way back down." He told me his father, Jim Brownlee, who is a well known collegiate coach in the baseball world, taught him that growing up. I have always tried to live my life in this fashion after I heard that, because I'm no different than anyone else out there. Some people dream of being a banker while others dream of being a lawyer. I, on the other hand, happened to dream of playing baseball. It doesn't matter which career path you choose, everyone has that one thing in common: they are chasing a dream.

Just because I am a professional baseball player doesn't mean I am any more special or different than other hard working person in any other professional field. What I like about the quote is it reinforces the notion that you can't step on other people to achieve your dreams. The last thing you ever want to do is use someone else as a stepping stone to get you where you want to go. At some point in your life you will come back down from the highs that your career takes you to and you will run into those same exact people you met on that climb up only now in a little different situation.

I don't know about you, but I plan on being the same person regardless of where I am at professionally in my life, which includes on the baseball field and off it. It's easy to get caught up in the fame and the glory and all of that kind of stuff. You see it happen to people all of the time. The thing you can't do is let that go to your head. Everyone needs to remember what got them to that point. It takes a lot of hard work, determination, discipline, and a lot of other people supporting you on your journey to get to where you want to go. Don't take advantage of people; rather, take advantage of the opportunities on your journey toward your dreams.

As much as we wanted to build on the early lead we had, the bottom of the fourth inning didn't work out like we had hoped. Celestino did a good job of keeping our hitters off balance and made quick work of us in the bottom half of the inning. Dwight Childs battled, but struck out swinging for the first out. Marcus Bradley came in and took a few good swings but ultimately flew out to Drew Hedman in left field for the second out. Delvi Cid then got jammed on an inside pitch and hit a soft pop up to Coyle at second base for the last out of the inning.

Just like that, the fourth inning was over. It seemed like the game was flying by but I was doing my very best to try to enjoy the experience. One of the best ways to enjoy a game and make it more fun is to have more runs than the opponent, and so far tonight, that was the case. Our team was pretty loose and it was turning out to be a great night for a ball game. The crowd was into the game from the start, and unlike most crowds, they hadn't lost interest in the game. It seemed that as each inning passed, they got a little louder. It was also one of those nights where you could get a good sweat going but yet it wasn't too ridiculously hot. I was feeling good, and after a few sips of water and Gatorade to replenish my fluids, I made my way out to second base for the start of the next inning.

Chapter 5

Hard Work Beats Talent When Talent Doesn't Work Hard

"There is no substitute for hard work." – Thomas Edison

"I know you've heard it a thousand times before. But it's true – hard work pays off. If you want to be good, you have to practice, practice, practice. If you don't love something, then don't do it."
– Ray Bradbury

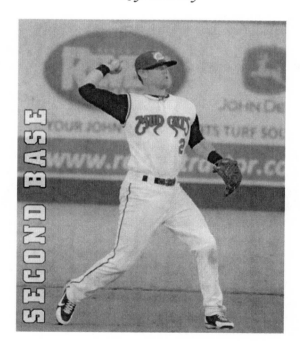

The top of the fifth inning always starts off with the dragging of the infield. Depending on which park you are playing, at different times during the game, the grounds crew drags the dirt on the infield. Sometimes it's in the top of the third inning and top of the sixth inning while at other places it's only once a game. At our park, it's only once a game and it is usually during the top of the fifth inning. Every infielder loves a clean smooth top layer of dirt allowing for perfect hops and great bounces and I'd say most infielders look forward to having it smoothed out in between innings.

For this game, the dragging of the infield dirt was kind of at a bad time for me. Having played most of the game in the outfield and then at first base up to this point, I hadn't had a chance to warm-up and take any ground balls in between innings. Sure, I was able to take a bunch in pre-game warm ups, but that was quite a few hours ago. Instead of being able to take all of my practice grounders on the dirt, I was forced to move in and take most of them on the infield grass because the grounds crew was busy tending to the infield dirt. The grass acts much differently than the dirt does, usually softening the hops and slowing the ball down quite a bit. Either way, I was forced to play the hand I was dealt. I was able to sneak a few in on the dirt right before the catcher's throw to second. Those few ground balls on the dirt eased my mind a little. It doesn't matter how many games you play or how many ground balls you take, it always nice knowing that you feel good and are prepared to play your position during the game.

I didn't get any action in the first four innings in the field, but it didn't take long for the ball to find me in the fifth. The first batter for Salem, Jayson Hernandez, took a 1-1 pitch and popped it up to the right side of the field. As soon as the ball was hit I got a good read and jump on it and drifted back into the outfield grass a few steps. I got under the ball and secured the catch and the first out of the inning. Just as with my single in the first inning I was able to let out a sigh of relief. Making the first play on a ball that comes to you always allows you to relax a little. It's always nice to get that one out of the way and the huge smile on my face was evidence of that. There were smiles and laughing all around the infield as we threw the ball around and got ready for the next batter.

I didn't have much time to relax when the next ball came my way. People always say when hits come they come in bunches, and apparently that saying goes for playing defense as well. The second batter of the inning, Lucas LeBlanc hit a decently hard hit ground ball just to the right of the pitchers' mound up the middle. I got a good read on it, made my way to my right and was able to backhand it just before the ball reached the outfield grass. I secured the ball, set my feet, and made a good throw to first base for the second out. I had to wait until the fifth inning to get any action in the field, but then consecutive batters found a way to hit the ball to me. It's funny how baseball works like that.

I was fully prepared for the next batter to hit the ball right at me, but that wasn't the case. Salem's James Kang, who was two for two heading into this at bat, grounded out to Ronny Rodriguez at short to end the inning. Jordan Cooper had yet again hung another zero up on the board and we took our three run lead into the bottom of the inning.

Baseball's a funny game. It's one of the only, if not the only game, where the defense is in control of the ball. It's a game where you will see managers and coaches in uniform with the rest of the players. It's a game where if you fail seven out of ten times at the plate, you're considered a good hitter. And it's a game where you can spend the entire nine innings at a position and not once get a ball hit your way. It's not like basketball where, on almost every possession, everyone touches the ball. Even though the ball might not get hit your way, you always have to be ready on every pitch for the ball to be shot your way.

In that fifth inning, when the balls were hit to me, I didn't have any second thoughts on what I should do or what I needed to do to field the ball and get an out. I have spent many years on the field with no one in the stands working on fielding ground balls and working on my swing in the cages. All I needed to do was just resort back to all of the hard work I had done and let my instincts take over, and that's exactly what I did and exactly what happened.

The single most important thing that any athlete can do is practice. The more time you put into something the better you become. I've heard people talk about the ten thousand hour rule, where in order to become a master of your craft you must spend at least that amount of time before you really are able to truly master whatever it is that you're doing. Ten thousand hours is little over four hundred and sixteen days. That's twenty four full hours a day for over four hundred and sixteen days. That's a lot of time to put toward something, but if you really want to get better and achieve your dreams, you have to put that kind of time and work in. I'm not saying you have to put in ten thousand hours of work, but just a few hours a day here and there will help tremendously.

One of the many things Brian Cain has taught me is that when investing your time, you want to do a little a lot, not a lot a little. It's much more effective to hit the gym, or the cage, or the field for an hour a day during the week than to show up only on Saturday for five hours. Baseball, like most things in athletics, is a game of repetition. Pitching and hitting are about trying to repeat your mechanics over and over in order to put yourself in the best position to have success time and time again.

The more repetitions you can give yourself and the more often you can practice those repetitions, the better off you will be as a player. If you show up once a week, even though it's for five hours, you won't be able to repeat your moves as well because of the amount of time in between your sessions. Think about it in school terms, would you retain and learn more information from a class that you had once a week or would it be easier to retain and learn more information from a class you had five times a week? The answer to that is easy, and it carries over to the athletic field. The more often you can practice something and the more repetitions of a specific athletic movement you practice, the better your chances are of doing that in a game. In stressful situations, such as games, your body resorts back to what you have trained it to do. If you have trained it properly there is no reason for you to think you won't experience success.

The other thing people always say when you talk about practice is that practice makes perfect. I don't know about you but I don't know any perfect people in my life, and I don't think I ever will. I don't like to think of practice in that way. Instead I like to say perfect practice takes over in perfect game opportunities. If you practice the right way, meaning you practice in a game-like atmosphere, there is no question it will translate over to the game. Will it allow for a perfect game? Probably not. But when the perfect opportunity arises, if you have properly prepared, you will be more than able to take advantage of it. No one can ever expect you to go and be perfect in a game every single time out, but there is no reason you can't strive to be perfect, and that starts in practice. If you allow yourself to have the correct mindset it allows you the opportunity for a bigger window for success during competition.

The whole reason I'm able to call myself a professional baseball player is due to my work ethic and practice mentality, not necessarily because of my talent level. Hard work beats talent when talent doesn't work hard: fittingly the name of this chapter. That saying couldn't be more true and I believe in it 100%. I have seen it happen time and time again. Throughout my entire life I have been blessed to play with and against some incredibly talented athletes and it's always the hard workers who are there in the end.

In high school I played football against many guys that ended up at Division 1 schools and top Division 2 schools. My high school baseball team yielded four Division 1 recruits with numerous junior college and other collegiate players. My youth soccer team growing up won a National Indoor Soccer Championship and had players on it who were drafted into the MLS and/or played overseas in Europe. My select baseball team growing up was filled with D-1 and professional players, one who even had the opportunity to play in the College World Series in Omaha. I have been around many talented kids my whole life, but it's not always the talented ones that make it to the next level, it's the ones who work their tail off who do.

I am a prime example of this. I'm not a flashy player. I'm not an imposing physical figure. I don't necessarily pass the eye test. I don't throw the ball 95 miles per hour across the infield. I don't hit 500 foot home runs. I'm, by no means, the fastest kid on the team. I also don't make web gems every time a ball is hit my way. But what I am, is a fundamentally sound ball player with a great work ethic, tremendous passion for the game, and the will to succeed at any cost.

The following list includes some of my accomplishments that I have achieved during my baseball career:

- 2011 Class A-Advanced Carolina League All-Star
- 2009 Pre-Season Collegiate All-American
- Three-Time All-Big Ten
- Two-Time All-Region
- University of Iowa Record Twenty-Five Game Hitting Streak
- Second Place All-Time for Hits In a Season at the University of Iowa with 87
- 2005 Louisville Slugger Iowa High School Player of the Year
- 2005 Bob Feller Iowa Class 4A Pitcher of the Year
- 2005 Iowa Class 4A First Team All-State Captain
- Two-Time Iowa Elite All-State Team
- Three-Time First Team All-State

Now I am not sharing this list of accomplishments with you to try and brag about myself. I am sharing this list with you to show you what a kid with a little talent can do when he works extremely hard. You don't have to be extremely talented to do these kinds of things. All it takes is a dream, a determination, and a lot of hard work. Anything is possible if you set your mind to it.

Many college teammates of mine at the University of Iowa were much more talented than I was. I was one of the last players in the 2005 recruiting class to sign with the Hawkeyes and I'm the last one still playing in professional baseball from that class. The reason for that isn't because of talent, but rather the time and work I have put in. My college coach, Ryan Brownlee, helped to push me in college and I owe a lot of where I am today to him pushing me to become a better player. I showed up to college thinking that I had everything figured out, but when I showed up on campus, my eyes were opened up to a whole new world. I wasn't a highly recruited kid who was given a large scholarship and had everything handed to me. I had to work to earn respect from my teammates and coaches. Along the way, I developed a chip on my shoulder that to this day has never left.

The following chart lists the chances athletes have to move on to the next level. This chart, courtesy of the National Collegiate Athletic Association, shows the probability of an athlete moving on from one level to the next in their careers.

	Men's Basketball	Women's Basketball	Football	Baseball	Men's Ice Hockey	Men's Soccer
High School (Total)	535,289	435,885	1.095M+	474,219	35,732	411,757
High School Seniors	152,940	124,539	313,141	135,491	10,209	117,645
NCAA (Total)	17,890	16,134	69,643	31,999	3,891	22,987
NCAA Freshman	5,111	4,610	19,898	9,143	1,112	6,568
NCAA Seniors	3,976	3,585	15,476	7,111	865	5,108
NCAA Drafted	51	31	253	693	10	37
HS to NCAA	3.3%	3.7%	6.4%	6.7%	10.9%	5.6%
NCAA to Pro	1.3%	0.9%	1.6%	9.7%	1.2%	0.7%
HS to Pro	0.03%	0.02%	0.08%	0.51%	0.10%	0.03%

Note: These percentages are based on estimated data and should be considered approximations of the actual percentages. Last Updated: September 17, 2012

Chart Courtesy of NCAA.org

I took a few sports psychology classes as a psychology major in college and in one of my classes this chart came up. My particular teacher made it a point to show the class, most of which were athletes, how hard it is to move on from high school to college, and then from college to professional sports. If you look at the numbers, baseball has the highest rate of high school athletes someday reaching the professional ranks, at 0.51%. That's saying that roughly only five out of every one thousand high school baseball players will make it one day as a professional. If you look at the chart you'll see the other percentages for moving up among the major sports in America.

I don't want you to look at this chart and be discouraged. Remember what I said earlier. If it was easy everyone would do it. You might not be the most talented kid, but with a little bit of talent and a lot of hard work you can go places. I know this because I am doing it right now. I am proud to say I am one of the 0.51% of high school baseball players who now is still playing professionally and part of the 9.7% of collegiate players who made it to pro ball. I would also say that of the 995 people that didn't make it from high school to professional baseball or the 903 who didn't make it from college to pro ball; many of them were probably much more talented than I was.

My goal has always been to make it to the big leagues, and I am striving to one day make it there. I am fighting for one of only seven hundred and fifty spots that are available on Major League rosters. The odds aren't necessarily in my favor, but neither were the odds to make it from high school to college or from college to the pros. Just because the odds might not be in your favor doesn't mean that you can't do it. If you work hard and have the right mind set anything is possible.

The best part about hard work and busting your butt is when it pays off. Anyone who has ever spent the hours in the gym busting their butt to get better knows what I am talking about. There aren't any special remedies, there aren't any secret shortcuts, and there aren't any hidden secrets to reaching your dreams. The only way to achieve your goals and achieve your dreams is through hard work and hard work alone. It's not easy, but again, if it was easy everyone would do it.

I'll say it again; hard work beats talent when talent doesn't work hard. Hard work is the deciding factor in the success athletes have. Sure a talented kid may have a lot of success early on in his or her career, but how many times have you seen an athlete get caught or passed by their peers because his or her peers have worked harder than the more talented athlete. It happens all the time. Whatever it is you want to do with your life, work hard at it. If you practice the right way, do a little a lot, not a lot a little, and outwork your opponents you will have an opportunity to experience a lot of success in life.

It had appeared that all of my hard work was paying off and carrying over into this game. I had singled offensively and fielded the ball cleanly when it was hit to me at all of my positions. Heading into the bottom of the fifth inning we had encountered our fair share of success as a team. Once back in the dugout I got some ribbing from teammates after making the first few plays I had a chance on in the game. Our Mudcats' team this year was pretty close, and we never missed out on a chance to give each other a hard time. A few pitchers were telling our hitters we needed to put up more runs because I was coming in to pitch. I even heard someone say no lead was safe when you have a position player closing out the game. I enjoyed the comments and everyone laughed. I think I enjoyed the comments because they were right; there's never such thing as too big of a lead.

Tony Wolters led off the bottom of the fifth for us. He didn't have a hit so far in the game, but he did reach base back in the first inning with a walk. He was quickly the first victim of the inning with a pop out to third base. I followed Wolters with a ground out to Salem's second baseman Sean Coyle. Giovanny Urshela, who hit a big home run on his last at bat back in the third inning, then followed as the third out of the inning. Gio hit a hard ground ball but it was right at James Kang at shortstop. We went one, two, three in the bottom of the fifth inning. We just couldn't find a way to build on our lead.

Despite giving up a few runs in the second and third innings, Salem's Miguel Celestino did a good job of keeping us off the scoreboard in the middle innings. The fifth inning was his last of the evening and closed the book on him for the game. He threw five innings, gave up three hits, three earned runs while walking three and striking out three. The two pitches I am sure he would want back were the double by Cid in the second inning and the home run by Gio in the third inning. Besides those he pitched a pretty solid game. Having not scored any runs, we carried that three run lead over into the sixth inning.

Chapter 6
Believe In Yourself

"It's not who you are that holds you back, it's who you think you're not."
— Anonymous

"There are people out there who tell you you can't. What you've got to do is turn around and say 'watch me.'" — Unknown

I couldn't have been more excited for the sixth inning to start. Having grown up as a shortstop, I couldn't wait to get back to my favorite position. Not only was it cool for me to move around and play different positions all night, but it allowed for a few of my teammates to do the same. In the fifth inning when I was at second base, Tony Wolters slid over and played third for an inning. Now that I was at shortstop, Ronny Rodriguez moved over and held down the position for an inning. Neither of the two guys were third basemen, as they both played everyday up the middle, so it was cool they got to experience a little change of scenery. I think they both would tell you they enjoyed the experience.

As a result of Ronny and Tony playing up the middle I wasn't able to see much action at shortstop throughout the season in Carolina. I always spend time in pre-game and Spring Training getting my ground balls in to make sure I am ready at each position, but I wasn't able to put myself in a true game-like situation much during the season. I was able to play a handful of games at shortstop for our AAA affiliate in Columbus, but that was way back in late April. Despite the lack of games over there I wasn't worried at all. I was excited to get out there and give it a go.

Jordan Cooper was still on the mound for us, and he continued in the sixth inning what he had done in the previous five innings. Michael Almanzar did leadoff the inning with a line drive single, but that was all of the damage that would be done. Brandon Jacobs followed with a fly out to our rightfielder, Drew Hedman struck out swinging, and Sean Coyle grounded out to me at short to end the inning. Almanzar did manage to mix in a stolen base, but wasn't able to get past second base. Coop shut the door once again on the Red Sox as he had amassed six shutout innings and counting.

The ground ball that Coyle hit to me was hit decently hard and a few steps to my right in the hole. I backhanded it after a good hop and made a good throw over to first. It's one of those plays you picture in your head over and over. You picture yourself taking your time, taking a couple shuffles, and firing a bullet across the diamond for the out. I'd like to say I fired a bullet across the infield, at least it felt like that, but either way, the throw beat the runner for the last out of the inning. It felt just like old times and I'm pretty sure everyone could see the big smile on my face after I made the play and jogged towards the dugout.

Like I said earlier, growing up I was always a shortstop. It wasn't until college that I played second base, and it was at second base where everyone always seemed to think I was destined to stick. I didn't have an outstanding arm and I was quick with turning double plays, so a lot of people felt second base was a natural fit. After my sophomore year of college, our shortstop Jason White graduated and moved on to the Baltimore Orioles organization. Typically, after this happens your second baseman will slide over to short unless you have a really talented underclassman or a recruit who can step in and do the job. Despite not having any underclassman win the job, heading into my junior year I was still the starting second baseman, not the shortstop.

I will admit that part of the reason I didn't start the season at shortstop was because I didn't play the position very well during fall ball. I also will agree that second base is probably my best position, but I still believe that I can get the job done at short. After two different guys spent some time at shortstop early in the season, I found myself over there for a Saturday double-header at Indiana. After those games, I went on and played that position for the rest of the season and every game my senior year before my arm injury. I always believed I could play over there. It just took me some time to prove it to everyone else.

I have mentioned before in this book that I'm a firm believer that anyone can accomplish anything they want to and set their mind to. The first step in doing that is to believe in yourself. If you don't have confidence in yourself or believe in yourself how can you ever expect anyone else to? When you completely buy into something the sky is the limit on what you can accomplish. The impossible becomes possible, the unexpected is expected, and you are able to tell all of the doubters that you did what they said you couldn't do. There is no better feeling in the world than that.

A lot of people didn't think I would make it as a college baseball player. Some of those people included my good friends, my teammates, opposing players, fans, parents, scouts and even some college coaches. People were just waiting for me to stumble and be able to tell me they told me so. I was bound and determined that I wasn't ever going to let that happen. Since high school I have accomplished many things in my career including playing in every level of professional baseball except the big leagues. I'm even proud to say I have played shortstop in AAA.

In the recruiting process there were a few college coaches who were apprehensive about me and as a result didn't offer me a scholarship or recruit me very hard. Some of those schools are very close to my home town and schools that I played numerous times during my college career. After playing those schools for the final time my senior year, there was no better feeling than having those coaches tell me I turned myself into a great ballplayer and that they made a mistake in not recruiting me and getting me on their campus. I have even had a coach tell me the biggest mistake he has ever made as a coach was not recruiting me enough to get me on his campus. Being told those things, coming from the same people who told me they weren't sure I had the ability to play at the next level, meant a lot to me. I always believed in my abilities and it felt good knowing they finally saw those abilities and talents as well.

I always wanted to be a professional athlete. I always idolized athletes on TV and dreamed of one day being as good as they were and seeing myself on TV. During my junior year in college, my hitting coach, Ryan Brownlee, put a piece of athletic tape in my helmet with a saying written on it. The saying was, "Be who you are, stay with what made you good." I never quite exactly understood what it meant until I got into professional sports. In college I always felt I had to be perfect and couldn't make mistakes because I perceived professional athletes as perfect, flawless people who never make mistakes. Boy was I ever wrong.

When you flip on ESPN and see all of the amazing highlights from all the different games you instantly think that those guys and girls are in another world. What I learned was that yes, they are extremely talented, but at the same time they aren't any different than anyone else. A lot of people think of professional athletes as being these special one-of-a-kind talents where everything comes easy to them. I'm here to tell you that's not necessarily the case. They're just normal people like anyone else. In college, I was always too busy trying to be perfect in game situations and like we've talked about before, no one is perfect. In baseball, you fail much more than you succeed and the first step to having success is realizing that failure is part of the game. While I was trying to be perfect I was actually hindering my development as a player.

I have a lot of friends playing in the Major Leagues and obviously they are talented, but they put their shoes on one shoe at a time just like anyone else. All of those guys have worked extremely hard to get where they are. They are the best athletes in the world, yet they still make mistakes and learn from them just like everyone else. The one thing that sets them apart from other players is that they believe in their abilities and they believe they can accomplish anything. When they do make mistakes they realize that it's part of the game and they don't let that shake their confidence. Even if they have had four strikeouts on the day they will still have the confidence in themselves to want the bat in their hands with the game on the line in the ninth inning. The biggest separation from elite athletes and everyone else is the mental game. The talent differences are very small between the Major Leagues and the minors, but the mental game differences are huge.

What Coach Brownlee was trying to teach me with that note in my helmet was that I didn't have to be anyone else except myself. I didn't need to be a hero and try to be perfect, I just needed to make the routine plays and have good quality at bats. I needed to believe in myself and believe in my abilities. To this day that quote is my all time favorite. You'll find that quote up on my wall in my room at home as well as in the back of every locker I've ever used in professional baseball as you can see on the next page.

BE WHO YOU ARE, STAY
WITH WHAT MADE YOU GOOD!

Having played with and against some of the best baseball players in the world, it's always amazing to hear the stories about what people have overcome in their careers. As I said before, many people think college athletes or professional athletes have traveled easy roads to get where they have gotten and that everything has come easy to them. Although sometimes that can be the case, it isn't the norm. Everyone has had a past and almost everyone has overcome something while chasing their dreams.

One of my good friends that I have played with in the Cleveland Indians system, Donnie Webb, is a great example of someone who has believed in himself when other people have not. He's a switch hitting outfielder who was drafted by the Indians in the tenth round of the 2008 MLB Draft out of Oklahoma State. He's currently a member of the Miami Marlins Organization and has played as high as AAA. Before he was drafted he started out at a Division II school before he transferred to OSU. Would it surprise you to know that he was cut from his high school team? I sure was surprised when he told me.

What Donnie did and many other athletes do when they reach a tough stretch in their career is dig down deep and believe. Nothing tells a player that someone doesn't think they are good enough more than getting cut from a team. It's no doubt a terrible feeling, but don't ever let that keep you from continuing toward your dreams. In today's world everyone will tell you what you can't do. People are always told they are too short, too small, too slow, not strong enough, don't throw hard enough, can't jump high enough, aren't smart enough, or are flat out not good enough. Just because someone says that stuff doesn't mean you can't work hard and change that perception.

Everyone has heard Michael Jordan's story. Much like Donnie, he was cut from his high school team and he went on to become arguably the best basketball player ever to play the game. James

Harrison, a linebacker from the Pittsburgh Steelers, went undrafted and signed with the Steelers as an undrafted free agent. Harrison has since won a couple Super Bowls and been named to numerous Pro Bowls. Kurt Warner was an undrafted free agent signee in the NFL as well. He's since been named MVP and Super Bowl MVP. He didn't let going undrafted affect his success. Many other great players weren't drafted into the NFL either, guys like Wes Welker, Adam Vinatieri, Antonio Gates, and Arian Foster.

Frank Hermann, a pitcher in our Cleveland Indians system, who has been up and down between the Major Leagues and AAA the past few years went undrafted and signed with the Indians as an undrafted free agent. In baseball, you also see many guys get drafted by one team, released at some point, and make it to the Major Leagues with another team. Just because someone or an organization says you can't do something, doesn't mean you can't eventually do it. Your time will come if you work hard and believe in yourself.

All of the athletes I've named in the previous paragraphs didn't let obstacles get in their way and stop them from chasing their dreams. These guys are great examples that you can be successful even if you aren't drafted or even if you get cut from a team at some point in your life. A lot of athletes will tell you that they learned the most about themselves during the tough times and times of struggle. I didn't have a lot of success during my freshman year in college but that was the best thing that ever happened to me. It made me look in the mirror and dig down deep and figure out not only who I was as a player, but who I was as a person.

When people experience periods of struggle they either push through and get better or shut down and surrender. There's that popular saying: if you do what you've always done you will get the results you've always gotten. In order to make it over the hump when you struggle, you sometimes have to do things a little different. You might need to work a little harder, you might need to work on your weaknesses more, or you just might need to believe in yourself a little more and get rid of your self doubts. Whatever it is you do, push through the struggles and don't give up. I've never talked with someone about athletics who gave up and quit when things were hard, tell me when looking back on it that it was worth it to quit.

It takes a lot of hard work to make it to the top but it takes even more work once you reach the top to stay there. Before you can even attempt to make it to the top you have to believe that you deserve to be there. Another saying I've always loved is if you think you can you might, if you think you can't you're right. In other words, if you think positively and believe in yourself, you put yourself in a position to succeed. If you don't believe in yourself and don't think positive thoughts, you put yourself behind the eight ball and don't even give yourself a chance from the start.

The most overlooked part of athletic competition is the mental side. The mental aspects of sports separate the average players from good players and the good players from great players. Everyone worries about controlling their body and getting into the best physical shape possible. All of that is very important, but what controls your body? It's the six inches between your ears that controls the six feet below it. When you think positive thoughts and believe in yourself, the sky is the limit. Don't let road blocks and struggles get you down. Road blocks and struggles, things such as losing streaks, slumps, and injuries, are going to happen. They're all part of the game. The important thing to keep in mind is to remember that those roadblocks aren't barriers to keep you from achieving things but rather they are challenges to remind you and show you how badly you want something. Challenges push you to continue to believe in yourself and force you to continue to work hard towards your goals.

In the bottom of the sixth inning we had the heart of our lineup coming up. Ronny Rodriguez, Tyler Cannon, and Todd Hankins, our four, five, and six hitters, were due up. Charle Rosario was on the hill for Salem after taking over for Miguel Celestino. He quickly got to work and got the first out. Ronny hit a ground ball to Salem's shortstop James Kang and he made a good throw across the diamond just in time to beat Ronny to the bag. Tyler Cannon followed with the second out of the inning, striking out looking on a two-two pitch. Rosario recorded the first two outs with little problem.

The third batter of the inning, Todd Hankins, got a decent pitch to hit and was the first to reach base against Rosario. Todd hit an infield single that made for a tough play for the shortstop who fielded it but had no play. Todd's presence on the bases was short lived though as Dwight Childs took the second pitch he saw and flew out to Brandon Jacobs in center field. Rosario got out of the inning without any harm. We weren't able to push any more runs across the board to increase our lead.

I picked up my hat and glove and proceeded to make my way out to third base but not before I made sure to grab some Gatorade and water. With all of the excitement of the game and the events that were going on, I wanted to make sure I was hydrated and I didn't cramp up when I was pitching or catching. Our trainer and strength coach Jeremy Heller and Jake Sankal always do a good job of trying to keep us hydrated and feeling good during the warm summers in Carolina. Anyone who has ever been in North Carolina in mid July knows what I'm talking about with the heat. Luckily, it was August and the temperature was much cooler. Still, I still didn't want to take any chances. I also had a little bit more time than normal to take the field as I didn't have very far to run to get to my next position. Third base was just a hop, skip, and a jump away from our dugout. After downing the refreshing liquids I jogged out to my position and got myself ready for the seventh inning.

Chapter 7
Control What You Can Control

"You cannot control what happens to you, but you can control your attitude toward what happens to you..." – Brian Tracy

I moved over to the hot corner for the seventh inning. I felt confident heading over there as I had fielded all the previous ground balls hit to me successfully in the game. As I fired a few throws across the infield during warm ups, Salem's manager Billy McMillon made some small talk with me. I always enjoy playing third base as it gives me a chance to chat with the opposing team's third base coach in between innings. Usually the third base coach is the team's manager, but occasionally it will be their hitting coach. Anyone who knows me knows I love to talk and chat it up, so I always take advantage of this opportunity.

On this night Billy told me it was cool that I had the opportunity to play all nine positions. He asked me a little bit about my past like where I went to college and stuff and then we talked about my previous playing experience at different positions. Having played Salem quite a bit this season Billy knew about my versatility in the infield, but was curious about my outfield, pitching, and catching experience. I quickly gave him a little run down and smiled when I told him about my very limited catching experience. He told me that his guys were fired up for me to catch because they planned on stealing some bases. I laughed and told him no one has ever successfully stolen a base against me. Without hesitation he laughed right back. See, I could say that was true because I could count on about 3 fingers the times I have caught in my life and in those times no one had ever attempted to swipe a base on me. He wished me luck in the last few innings and said it was neat to be part of a cool event like this as it doesn't happen very often.

It was not only cool that my coaching staff, my teammates, and the Indians Organization were supportive in giving me the opportunity to play all over the field, but it was cool that the Salem Red Sox were supportive as well. Sometimes when you do something goofy, such as having position players pitch or have different people playing different positions, other teams take offense to it and see it as a slap in the face. I appreciated the fact that Salem enjoyed the festivities and I was also very grateful for Billy McMillon wishing me luck in the process.

Jordan Cooper was back out on the mound for us to start the seventh inning. He had cruised through the first seven innings without much trouble. We did have Rob Nixon stretching and starting to throw in the bullpen in case he was needed. This was going to be Coop's last inning regardless of how well it went, and Rob was for sure out on the hill for the eighth inning. Rob could possibly make an appearance in the seventh inning if for some reason Coop struggled and ran into trouble. Through six innings Coop had given up only five hits while recording five strikeouts without walking a single batter. Coaches and baseball people will always tell you that if you limit the free bases you give up, you will win baseball games. With Coop not walking anyone and us not making any errors defensively thus far, we had put ourselves in a great position to win this game.

David Renfroe led off the inning for Salem. Renfroe hadn't had a hit heading into this at bat, his third one of the night. He got a decent pitch to hit and smoked it into right field for a single. With the first runner aboard, Rob started to quicken his pace in the bullpen. As the next batter, David Chester was at the plate, Renfroe made a dash for second base. Luckily for us our catcher Dwight Childs threw a bullet right on the bag allowing for Tony Wolters to apply an easy tag for the first out of the inning. Coop then buckled down and got Chester with a strikeout and followed that up by getting Jayson Hernandez to ground out to me at third base.

The successful top of the seventh inning closed the book on Jordan Cooper for the evening. He pitched extremely well and kept the Salem hitters off balance all night. Coop's final stat line was as follows: seven innings pitched, giving up six hits, allowing zero walks, giving up zero earned runs, and notching six strikeouts. It was a heck of a performance by Coop who was in line to pick up his eighth win of the season if we were able to hold on and finish the game out.

The ball that Hernandez hit to me was smoked right at me. I barely had any time to put my glove down before the ball was already there. I guess that's why they call it the hot corner, as balls come at you pretty quickly. Playing over there you never are able to control how hard the balls get shot your way, all you can do is be ready with every pitch for something to come screaming your way.

In life and in baseball there are only so many things you can control. You can't control an umpire's call, you can't control opposing players making great plays against you, you can't control hitters hitting a good pitchers' pitch, you can't control whether or not balls are hit your way defensively, and you can't control coach and management decisions on playing time or situational game strategy. As hard as it is sometimes, you just have to let those things go. Instead of wasting your energy and time on things you can't control, focus on the few things you have 100% control of, which includes your attitude and your effort. If you focus on the things you can control not only will you save yourself some headaches, but you'll most likely get the results you've desired all along.

As I talked about earlier, I didn't get drafted after I broke my arm. Anyone who plays professional baseball knows that signing as a free agent doesn't give you the easiest or straightest path to the big leagues. Once I signed, I reported to Mahoning Valley, Cleveland's Short Season A affiliate. As I was told when I signed, I was there to be a back-up guy. I didn't play a whole lot from the start and only notched a few hits in thirty-two at bats. I only played in nine games in about a months' time before I was moved down to our rookie team in Arizona. In Arizona, I played much more regularly and as a result hit much better. My whole life I have always been a starter who played pretty much every game. When I became a back-up guy I realized how tough it was to hit when you didn't see action and live pitching every game. Any back-up guy or anyone who doesn't play regularly will tell you as a hitter it's a battle to keep your timing.

Knowing that my role in the organization was as a back-up guy I had to try and find a way to get on the field more. The more often I was on the field the better I hit. Instead of complaining and worrying about things I couldn't control, things like the organization's thoughts about me as well as my manager and coaches playing time decisions, I focused on what I could control. I talked with Travis Fryman, who was my manager in Mahoning Valley, and asked him what I needed to do in order to get more playing time. I made it clear that I understood my role within the team and the organization, but that I wasn't just going to be happy with that. If that's what my role was, that was fine, but I was bound and determined to get on the field more often. My dream has always been to make it to the Big Leagues, and now that I was in professional baseball I wasn't just going to settle for being a back-up. His quick response was something that changed my life as a baseball player. Travis told me that I needed to learn how to play as many positions as possible.

I couldn't control when my manager put my name in the lineup, but I could control the different ways that he could put my name in the lineup. In the previous chapters I have told you about the different ways I learned to play the outfield and first base and how I basically became a utility player. After having that conversation with Travis, I told him to teach me the ropes of playing third base. Travis was a shortstop in the Major Leagues who eventually moved over and had to learn how to play third base later in his career. He shared with me his knowledge and helped me to feel about as comfortable as you can over on the hot corner.

I did everything that I could to make myself as valuable to the Indians Organization as I could, being that I was a free agent and all. Some people are drafted high and given a lot of money and are therefore valuable to the organization. Other prospects are traded for established Major League players, thus giving them value to the team they are traded to. I fit into neither of those categories and so I tried to find something I could control in order to keep myself around for as long as possible. My way of being valuable was being a utility player.

A lot of people spend time in their lives worrying about things they can't control. My first couple years in professional baseball I played the game with the wrong mindset, I played to not get released. I was constantly worrying about what people thought of me as a player instead of worrying about what I needed to do to get better. It took until my third year to realize I needed to focus on taking it one day at a time and play with the mindset I was going to make it to the Big Leagues rather than to play with the mindset I did not want to get released. I couldn't control my batting average, I couldn't control when I was in the lineup and when I was in the lineup I couldn't control what pitches I saw. I couldn't control what anyone thought about me as a player but I could control busting my butt in between the lines and showing up to the field with a smile on my face every day, ready to work hard. It's no surprise that when I had the right attitude and worried about what I could actually control, I had one of my best seasons of baseball in my career. That season I was named a Carolina League All-Star.

Like I've talked about many times, baseball is an extremely mental game. It's a game where you can do everything absolutely right and not get any of the results that you want. That's why in baseball you can't focus on the results. A lot of people always talk about baseball in terms of batting average and statistics, but those aren't things you can really control 100%. What you can control is hitting the ball hard and having quality at bats. A quality at bat isn't necessarily getting a hit, but rather moving a runner over, hitting a ball hard, scoring a runner from third, taking a walk to get on base, getting hit by a pitch, little things like that. Just because you don't get a base hit doesn't mean you haven't had a quality at bat.

You can square up four balls and hit them as hard as ever right at the centerfielder for an out, or you can roll over and hit four swinging bunts down the third base line for base hits. If you're 4 for 4 you're going to be feeling pretty good about yourself even though you haven't necessarily had quality at bats. Kids who don't get a hit but hit the ball hard right at the centerfielder four times feel like they didn't hit well because the score book doesn't say they got any hits. If you look at the big picture, which one is the more desired result, hitting a ball hard or rolling a ball over? If you hit a ball hard more likely than not it will find a hole. If you focus on trying to hit seven out of ten balls hard, something you can control, your batting average, which you can't control, will take care of itself.

I know many athletes that get all wound up and upset over the recruiting process from high school to college as well as the process it takes to go from college to the professional level. A lot of that stems from things that you can't control. Everyone wants to be the top recruit and that one person all of the coaches and scouts have their eye one, but the chances of that realistically happening are slim. The best way to get noticed by people at the next level is to win games. When you win games people get excited, and when people are excited people talk. The more people talk, especially about an exciting team, the more people start to show up at games. The more people who show up at games the more opportunities you have as a player to be seen. Being an individual won't get you to the next level, but being a hard working team player will.

The more games you win as a team the longer your season lasts. If you're lucky enough to make it to your teams' regional games or the state tournament, it gives you a great opportunity to be seen on a big stage. Now you might be saying you can't control how far your team goes, but I'm here to tell you, you can. You can control that by setting the bar high for not only yourself but also for your team. If you take care of business on the practice field, in the weight room, and most importantly during the off season, you will set not only yourself up, but your team up for success.

One of the biggest mistakes kids make at the lower levels of competition is to think you can just pick up a basketball or bat and glove when the season rolls around and have success. A very select few are ever able to do that. You always hear kids who don't get as much playing time as they would like complain that the coach doesn't know what he's talking about and that they should be playing more. Instead of worrying and blaming the coach for everything, why don't you focus on what you can control, and that's getting better. The off season is a great time to improve your skills by going to camps, working with personal trainers, attending open gyms, going to the local YMCA and shooting hoops, or just playing catch outside with a buddy. As we talked earlier with hard work, the more you do something the better you become at it.

If you're a basketball player and you shot 25 free throws and 25 jump shots every day, can you imagine how much better you would get? Just think how much better you would get as a result of a few shots a day. Even better, the best part is that's something you can control. If you did that every day, in a week you would have shot 175 free throws and jump shots and in about a month it adds up to 700 free throws and 700 jump shots. In the course of an off season, which for high school kids is roughly about six or seven months, you would easily amass anywhere from 4,200 to 4,900 free throws and jump shots. Do you realize how much better that would make a player? It would only take about thirty minutes a day to complete that task, that's not asking for a lot of time.

If you improve your game over the off season and are consistently practicing at a high level you will find yourself getting more playing time. Don't worry about what the coach thinks because you can't control that. Instead, focus on what you can do as a player, and that's giving a great effort and having a great attitude. If you do those things, you will find yourself right where you want to be.

I am sure every single high school kid would love to play in college and every college kid would love to play professionally. I'm sure on every team there is at least one guy that college coaches and scouts come to watch. Now you can't control who the scouts come to see, but by showing up to play the right way on the field every day, you can control who they leave talking about. Just because a coach comes to see a certain someone play doesn't mean they can't notice you out on the field as well. I have known a lot of guys who have had star players on their team, and when scouts showed up to watch the star player, they played well and as a result were given college scholarships or drafted to play professionally.

In baseball, infield and outfield is the best time to showcase your skills. If a college coach or scout shows up they know for a fact they will see you get ground balls or fly balls and make throws during that time. They can't guarantee you will see action in a game, but it allows for them to get a taste of what you can do defensively. How many kids do you know who actually take infield and outfield seriously? The answer to that is probably not very many. Great teams and great players take great infield and outfield practice because they know how important it is not only for their future, but also how important it is to get them ready for the game.

The other thing too many kids, coaches, and parents get caught up in is the umpires or referees. The first thing you need to realize is that they are human just like the rest of us. They have one of the toughest jobs to do, because as I mentioned earlier, if they do a great job nobody notices them, but if they make some questionable calls everyone is all over them. Players are going to make mistakes in games, coaches will make mistakes, and officials will make mistakes as well. It's going to happen and you shouldn't worry about it because it's part of the game. Don't ever let a bad call mentally check you out of a game.

Great players, great coaches, and great teams overcome those types of things and don't let them bother them. Why get worked up about something that you know is going to happen. I guarantee you that if you felt an official was the reason you lost a game, you could go back and find areas within that game that you could have controlled that would have changed the outcome of the game. Areas such as making easy shots in basketball, limiting free bases and making routine plays in baseball, or making tackles and holding onto the ball in football. Officials may make calls in crucial parts of the game, but officials aren't the reason your team wins or loses games.

Back to the game. Thus far we had done a great job of controlling what we could control. We had played great defense and hadn't committed any errors, Coop didn't allow any free bases on walks, and we had taken advantage of good pitches with people in scoring position to drive them in. Heading into the bottom of the 7th inning, we were looking to push a few more runs across and extend our lead.

Our lineup due up in the seventh inning was our eight, nine, and leadoff hitters. Earlier in the game, in the second inning, we got our first couple runs from this part of the order, and we were hoping it could tack on a few more runs here late in the game. Marcus Bradley led off the inning for us. His first at bat he walked and would later come around and score. In his second at bat he flew out to leftfielder Drew Hedman. Marcus quickly found himself down in the count with two strikes and grounded out to second baseman Sean Coyle for the first out of the inning. Delvi Cid then followed with a strikeout. With two outs Tony Wolters came up to the plate. He took a couple of great swings but came up empty, only to fly out to Headman in left field to end the inning.

Charle Rosario worked a scoreless sixth and seventh innings for Salem. He allowed just one hit and struck out two batters he faced. He and Celestino did a great job keeping Salem in the game. We jumped out to an early lead after three innings but weren't able to tack anything on to that. Other than the two pitches to Giovanny and Delvi, the Salem pitchers had keep us off the scoreboard. Other than those two hits we had only mustered up two others, my single in the first inning and Todd Hankins infield single back in the sixth inning.

I ended the inning on deck which is usually not a big deal, but on this day it was. I usually just head to the dugout and grab my hat and glove and head to my position, but tonight I was scheduled to catch the eighth inning. Having not caught much in my life I didn't have a lot of experience putting the gear on. It took me a little while, but with the help of my teammates, we made sure the gear fit properly. I finally got it all on and jogged out behind home plate. Talk about being nervous. I don't think I had ever been more nervous in my life.

7th Inning Stretch

(Yes I know the seventh inning stretch is in-between the top of the seventh and the bottom of the seventh, but I couldn't just put this in the middle of a chapter, so just bear with me. I mean what's a book about a baseball game without a 7th inning stretch?)

Here's a picture with my dad in a high school game for Lewis Central
High School during my high school career.

This is a picture of me hitting in summer ball during the Northwood's League Season for the La Crosse Loggers.

This is a picture of me turning a double play during the Corridor Classic against Northern Iowa when I was at the University of Iowa.

Here's a snapshot of my pre-game interview with Darren Headrick,
courtesy of the Carolina Mudcats, before the game against the Salem
Red Sox on August 25th 2012.

This picture, also courtesy of the Carolina Mudcats, ran in many of the newspaper and online articles about the game. It's pretty cool because you can see all of the nine positions from the one game at the same time. It brought the game full circle for me the first time I saw it. I was fortunate enough to have someone at the game with a camera capture this night.

Here's a picture of me hitting on the night I played all nine positions. I was glad I was able to get a single in the bottom of the first inning and get that out of the way. This picture is courtesy of the Carolina Mudcats.

PLAYERS	INNINGS 1	2	3	4	5	6	7	8	9
GAME LINEUP BY POSITION - JUSTIN TOOLE TIME *SATURDAY AUGUST 25, 2012*									
WOLTERS	2B	2B	2B	2B	3B	2B	2B	2B	2B
TOOLE	RF	CF	LF	1B	2B	SS	3B	C	P
URSHELA	DH	DH	DH	DH	DH	DH	DH	DH	DH
RODRIGUEZ	SS	SS	SS	SS	SS	3B	SS	SS	SS
CANNON	1B	1B	1B	3B	1B	1B	1B	3B	3B
HANKINS	3B	3B	3B	LF	LF	LF	LF	LF	LF
CHILDS	C	C	C	C	C	C	C	1B	C
BRADLEY	LF	LF	RF	RF	RF	RF	RF	RF	RF
CID	CF	RF	CF	CF	CF	CF	CF	CF	CF

This is the inning by inning breakdown my manager Edwin Rodriguez made so everyone knew what position they would be playing each inning. I snapped a quick picture of it with my phone in the clubhouse before the game. It was pretty cool showing up to the field seeing everyone huddled around it figuring out what they had to do for the night.

Carolina Mudcats											
Player	Pos	AB	R	H	2B	3B	HR	RBI	BB	SO	AVG
Tony Wolters	2B-3B-2B	3	0	0	0	0	0	0	1	0	.260
Justin Toole	RF-CF-LF-1B-2B-SS-3B-C-P	4	0	1	0	0	0	0	0	0	.232
Giovanny Urshela	DH-1B	4	2	2	0	0	2	2	0	0	.277
Ronny Rodriguez	SS-3B-SS	4	0	0	0	0	0	0	0	1	.265
Tyler Cannon	1B-3B-1B-3B	3	0	0	0	0	0	0	1	1	.263
Todd Hankins	3B-LF	2	1	1	0	0	0	0	0	0	.231
Dwight Childs	C-1B-C	3	0	0	0	0	0	0	0	2	.155
Marcus Bradley	LF-RF	2	1	0	0	0	0	0	1	0	.143
Rob Nixon	P-RF	0	0	0	0	0	0	0	0	0	.000
Delvi Cid	CF-RF-CF	3	0	1	1	0	0	2	0	1	.281

This is a clip of the online box score, courtesy of MILB.com, for our team after the game. Pretty cool seeing all of those positions next to my name.

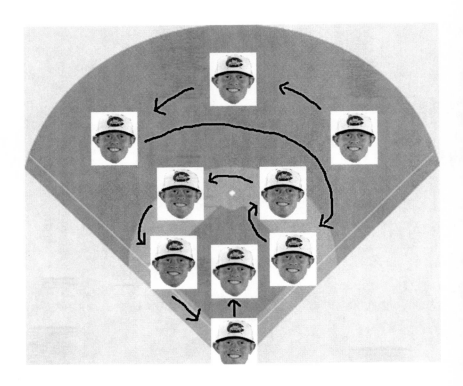

Here's a cool picture which shows not only the different positions I played but also the order in which I did so.

This picture, courtesy of the Carolina Mudcats, would show up on the scoreboard after every inning and my head would pop up in a new position. This allowed the fans to keep closer tabs on what was going on in the game and what positions I had played.

I teamed up with Fresh Brewed Tees out of Cleveland, Ohio and created a shirt based on the game. You can check out the shirt and pick one up at <u>http://freshbrewedtees.com/product/details/480</u>. The picture is courtesy of Fresh Brewed Tees.

Here's a picture of Five County Stadium in Zebulon, North Carolina, home of the Carolina Mudcats.

Here's a team photo of the 2012 Carolina Mudcats courtesy of the Carolina Mudcats. Class A Advanced Affiliate of the Cleveland Indians. This night wouldn't have been possible without these guys and the Cleveland Indians Organization.

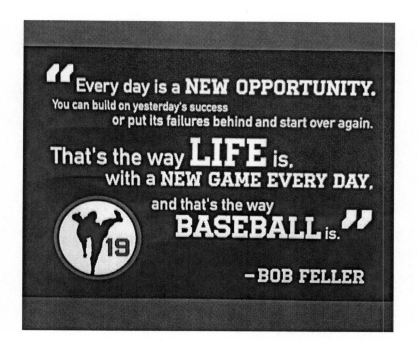

This is a picture of Bob Feller's quote that is up in the Cleveland Indians' weight room at our Spring Training and Player Development Complex in Goodyear, Arizona.

Chapter 8
Be Comfortable Being Uncomfortable

"Be willing to be uncomfortable. Be comfortable being uncomfortable. It may get tough, but it's a small price to pay for living a dream."
– Peter McWilliams

The top of the eighth inning had finally arrived and I found myself catching warm up pitches from Rob Nixon. It was the inning that I was most worried about. Although it wasn't the right thing to do, in my head I was playing through all of the terrible things that could go wrong. Of all the positions I was playing today this is the one that had been on my mind the most. I knew heading into the game that I would be catching and then pitching the last two innings and the last thing I wanted to do was blow the game. Coop had pitched a heck of a game and I wanted to preserve the win. I was hoping we would have a big lead by the time I came in to catch and pitch, but I wouldn't say a three run lead is a big one.

As I caught the warm up pitches the umpire behind home plate, Jansen Visconti, asked me about my catching experience. I don't think he was too comfortable hearing that I had done this only a few times. As an umpire it's always comforting knowing that your catcher can block balls in the dirt and keep him from getting hit as much as possible. My lack of experience definitely didn't settle any of his nerves. When Rob told me he was ready I made the signal for the throw to second base. I was pumped to see how this whole throwing down to second thing went and as the ball came I popped up and delivered a strike right on the bag. I actually even impressed myself with how good of a throw it was.

My experience as a catcher, like I said, is extremely limited. I think I've caught maybe three times that I can remember. The first two were when I was younger, around eleven or twelve. I caught just a few games for my select team, the Omaha Pacesetters, but it never materialized into anything. My mom hated me being back there, just about as much as she hated me playing football, and was relieved that the position didn't turn into a long term thing. My most recent experience behind the dish was back in the summer of 2006 after my freshman year in college. For the last game of our summer collegiate league, we drew positions out of a hat. I happened to draw catcher, and caught the first five innings. It wasn't too crazy and to be honest, nothing really stuck out about the experience. Only a couple people reached base and nobody tried to steal. The best part of the experience was that nobody scored any runs.

I was fortunate to have Rob Nixon on the mound for this inning. He was the type of pitcher who didn't throw too ridiculously hard, low to mid 90's, but was able to hit his spots and locate really well. Having pitched quite a bit in high school and then in college, I was fairly confident in my abilities to call a game. It was cool that Edwin let me call the eighth inning. Thinking back on it he probably let me because I didn't know any of the signs he would have used to relay in to me what pitches he wanted to be thrown.

The top of the order was up for Salem, and the first batter of the inning was leadoff hitter Lucas LeBlanc. As he stepped up to the plate he told me he thought it was pretty cool I was back there catching and able to play all these positions. I responded with a thank you but don't think you're getting any fastballs for that. He laughed along with the home plate umpire and we got ready for the first pitch. As Rob started his delivery I noticed I was really close to home plate. Luckily for me I didn't get hit as Lucas fouled off the first pitch. To be honest I don't know how he didn't just hit me in the back of my head with his swing. I was way too close. I looked over to the dugout and everyone was motioning me to move further back. I scooted back, checked my distance from the hitter and instantly felt much better.

Rob buckled down and delivered the next pitch for a strike. We were up in the count early but a ball, a foul ball, and another ball brought the count to two and two. I really didn't want anyone to reach base because my chances of blocking anything in the dirt and throwing anyone out were slim. I almost felt like a runner on base was an automatic run. Lucky for me Rob threw a fastball that was a little up in the zone that LeBlanc barely nicked with his bat. I was completely surprised when the ball ended up in my glove. LeBlanc struck out on a foul tip and I hopped up out of my crouch and threw it around the infield. There was one out and I was a third of the way through the inning.

The next batter for Salem was James Kang. He had already amassed two hits this evening and was looking for another. The first pitch was a ball. The second pitch was a ball. The third pitch was also a ball. One more ball and the speedy shortstop was on base. Rob focused in and delivered a strike on the fourth pitch of the at bat. There were three balls and one strike when Rob threw another good pitch and Kang put a good swing on it. He hit it hard, but right at Marcus Bradley in right field. There were now two outs.

The third batter for Salem in the top of the eighth inning was Michael Almanzar. Having played against Almanzar for the past couple of years I knew that he jumped on a lot of first pitch fastballs. Rob threw a curveball in there on the first pitch and Almanzar watched it go by for strike one. The next pitch was fouled off followed by two consecutive balls outside of the zone. With a two ball and two strike count, Rob threw another good curveball that Almanzar swung over the top of and I was just able to snag it before it hit the ground for out number three. Just like that the top of the eighth inning was over. I don't think the inning could have gone any better. Two strikeouts and a fly out and the Carolina Mudcats were a good defensive top half of the 9th inning away from a victory.

About a week before this game Edwin told me the only conditions I had to meet in order to pitch and catch was that I had to catch two bullpens and I had to throw two bullpens. The pitching was no problem but the catching was a little different. First I had to borrow some equipment from my teammates. Thanks to catchers Tyler Cannon and Dwight Childs, I was able to assemble some gear and a glove that worked. Anyone who has ever used anyone else's equipment knows how uncomfortable that can be. Now pair that with playing a whole new position you're not familiar with and you have the definition of being uncomfortable.

My mind was racing as I thought about catching prior to the game. I thought back to all of the things Brian Cain had taught me and the different things I learned in college about sports psychology. Brian always used the saying be comfortable being uncomfortable. The easier it is for you to get comfortable being in an uncomfortable situation the better you will perform. Take hitting for example. You can take as many swings in the cage or in batting practice, but the first time you step into the batter's box your heart will race and you'll feel a little uncomfortable. That nervousness and anxious feeling you get as an athlete before competition always makes you feel a little different. The quicker and easier you get accustomed to and comfortable with that, the better off you are as an athlete.

As I've talked about previously, I'm a utility player. It's cool that I am able to bounce around the organization and fill needs as a result of that, but being a utility player isn't glamorous by any means. You aren't the player who gets the headlines or puts up the big numbers. In order to stick around you have to do all of the little things right and do a lot of the dirty work that doesn't get much attention. As a utility player you might even have to pack up your belongings on short notice and fly to another city and meet up with another team. I know this from experience. I've had trips planned by my family and girlfriend at the time to come see me that got cancelled because just before they were scheduled to visit I got sent up or down to another team at a different level in a distant city.

As a utility player it's sometimes tough showing up to the field not knowing what position you might be playing, or if you are even playing at all. You might hit one day in the second spot, the next day in the ninth spot, and the following day in the seventh spot. The life of a utility player is constantly changing and you don't really know what to expect when you show up to the field every day. As a player I have had to learn how to be comfortable being uncomfortable because of the position I am in. It was either I learn how to do it or I was out of a job and out of baseball. I was never very good at being comfortable in uncomfortable situations, but I will say that since I have learned how to do it I've become a much better player.

One way you can help make the uncomfortable comfortable is by developing a routine. When many people step up to home plate they do so without a plan or anything to help them get their minds in the right spot and get them ready to go. As a hitter your main goal is to try and repeat your mechanics time and time again. Then when you get a good pitch the mechanics take over and you are able to hit the ball hard. Do you think you are able to perform effectively when your body feels different than when you practice? You might, but probably not very often. Routines can also be used for pitching and fielding.

Routines will get you in the right spot mentally to have success physically.

If you ever watch basketball players shoot free throws or ask them what they do before they shoot (their routine) they will be able to tell you the exact things they do. They know the number of bounces with the ball, the rhythm their body has, and what they focus on before they shoot. But if you think about baseball, how many people have a plan or routine like that when they step up to the plate? A routine at home plate can be as simple as taking a deep breath as you step in the batters' box and then tapping the middle and corner of the plate with the end of your bat. Some people like to dig holes for their back foot, others like to smooth out the dirt in the box, and still others might not even mess with the dirt at all. Whatever it is you feel comfortable with is fine. Nobody but yourself can tell you what your routine should be. Chances are there are even some people who have a routine without even knowing that they do.

Whatever you choose and are comfortable with in terms of your routine, make sure that when you step into the batter's box you make the box yours. Working with Brian, he always told me and my college teammates to own the box, to make it our own. He would also tell us, as we walked to the plate to get big, act big. The more confidence you can bestow upon yourself the more chance you have of success. Also, the more you practice a routine, the more comfortable you will start to feel in the batter's box. In turn, the more comfortable you start to feel in the box, the easier it will be for you to repeat your mechanics, thus allowing you more of a chance for success. The pitchers job is to try and make the hitter feel as uncomfortable in the batter's box as possible, while the hitter is trying to do the exact opposite. The more you practice a routine, the more comfortable you will get and the more successful you will be repeating your swing.

Having a routine doesn't just start when you get into games or batting practice, it starts when you start swinging in practice. That includes tee work, soft toss, front toss, and any other drills where you are swinging a bat. Now I understand with practice you don't always have as much time as you would like, but that doesn't mean you can't shorten your routine a little bit to fit within the time frame you have. I, for example, have a pretty lengthy routine at the plate, but when I hit off a tee or front toss I shorten it all and merely tap the center of the plate and inside corner of the plate before every swing. I will step out between swings, and take my time; I won't just get in there and see how many swings I can take in five minutes. Sometimes quantity work can be good, but more times than not you want to focus on the quality of the swings you take.

Routines not only work for baseball, but many other sports as well. The whole goal of an athlete is to feel comfortable in an uncomfortable game-like situation, and routines help to do that. You see golfers, bowlers, field goal kickers, soccer players, gymnasts, and just about any other athlete you can think of use routines. They use them because they work.

Another way you can help yourself as an athlete to feel comfortable in an uncomfortable situation is to do what I've been taught, known as fake it 'til you make it. What fake it 'til you make it means is that you go about your business with a confidence and a positive swagger. For example, if you show up to the field and you don't feel great, fake it. Be the guy on the field playing with energy and before you know it your body will follow. Your body always does what the mind tells it, and if you tell it you feel good and you act like you feel good, you eventually will get to the point where you feel good. Your teammates won't know that you don't feel your best, your coaches won't know, but they will build off of your positive energy. It only takes a little spark to start a huge fire, and it only takes a little energy for it to spread to the entire team.

A great example I've taught about fake it 'til you make has to do with pitching. As a pitcher in the Major Leagues, you'll get roughly thirty starts or so during a season. For about ten of those starts you will have your best stuff, for about ten other starts you will feel terrible, and for the other ten of your starts you will feel so-so. It's during those twenty games, especially the so-so games, where you don't feel you're at your best, that your season is made. You won't always show up to the field with your best stuff, and when that happens you have to find a way to battle though it.

Ok now, let's say you're pitching and you show up to the field and during warm-ups you don't have your best stuff. The only way to get yourself right back on track is to fake it 'til you make it. If you act differently on the mound or throw a few balls and get angry with yourself, the hitter and the opposing team will take notice. For example, if you throw a ball up and in at a hitter and he gets out of the way and you're upset with yourself, what's that tell the hitter? It tells him you didn't want to throw that pitch there. Now let's say you throw a pitch up and in at a hitter accidentally but you act the part and look like you meant to do that. What's the hitter thinking now?

In the first instance, the hitter knows you're not trying to come inside and can sit comfortably in the box and wait to hit a pitch the other way. In the second instance, the hitter has to now be ready to hit an inside pitch and an outside pitch, because as far as he's concerned you have no problem coming inside. He's also thinking in the back of his head that you aren't afraid to hit him. The hitter's reaction to the same pitch in that situation is different only because of the way the pitcher acted. The lesson from this is that if you can fake it and keep battling out there, you will put yourself in a spot to be successful, even if you don't necessarily have your best stuff.

When I got called up to AAA earlier in the year, I can't tell you that I was super comfortable in the situation. Due to an injury I found myself starting at shortstop after only playing there once during spring training. A lot of my teammates were big leaguers as were a lot of the guys on the opposing team, including the pitchers I was about to face in the next few days. I used the fake it 'til you make it method and found myself feeling comfortable. As a result, I had a lot of success. A lot of people can't tell what you're thinking or what you're feeling. If you look confident and act confident, the message you send to others is confidence. If you look scared and act scared, the message you send is that you're scared. Next time you show up to a competition or a game, it doesn't matter what sport, act big and carry yourself with confidence. I guarantee that if you do that it will take some wind out of the sails of your opponent. By doing so, even if you aren't necessarily confident heading into that game, your opponent will think you are.

While catching in the top of the eighth inning I definitely faked the part of being a catcher. I'd like to think that maybe it was because of the confidence I had in myself that I could do a good job behind the plate that Rob was able to throw a good inning. Pitchers will always tell you it's not fun throwing to someone who isn't a good catcher. I couldn't imagine what he was thinking having to throw to me, but the inning couldn't have turned out any better.

We were three outs away from winning the game, but before I could think about warming up in the bullpen I had to leadoff our half of the eighth inning. It wasn't necessarily the most convenient time to hit, as I would have enjoyed throwing as many pitches in the bullpen as I could have to get ready for the next inning. Nonetheless, I found myself in the batter's box against Salem's new pitcher Pete Ruiz. With a three run lead, any insurance runs to help the cause would be greatly appreciated.

I swung at the first pitch I saw from Ruiz and promptly grounded out to Michael Almanzar at third base for the first out. I would have loved to get a hit but at the same time I was relieved I could now head to the bullpen and warm-up. I made my way to the dugout and quickly grabbed my glove and headed to get loose. I watched from the bullpen as Giovanny Urshela headed to the plate. Gio was one for three with the big home run back in the third inning. Ruiz threw the first two pitches outside the strike zone. Way ahead in the count, Gio took advantage of the next pitch he saw and crushed it over the left field wall for his second home run of the game.

Even though the pitchers were rousing me during the game that we needed more runs because I was closing out the game, I was still pretty confident I could come in and throw a good ninth inning. Even with that, I can't argue with wanting to score more runs. A four run lead is much better than a three run lead, especially against a team like Salem who had scored quite a few runs on us during the season.

Okay just for the record; let me set things straight that I wasn't agreeing with the pitchers, I just understood where they were coming from.

As I continued to warm-up in the pen, Ronny Rodriguez stepped up to the plate. Ronny hadn't recorded a hit in his previous three at bats tonight, and his fourth wasn't much better. With a three ball and one strike count, Ronny popped up to Salem's second baseman Sean Coyle. With two outs, Tyler Cannon came up. Tyler put together a great at bat, fighting off some tough pitches. The count was full when he hit a pitch well, but it was right at rightfielder Lucas LeBlanc for the third and final out of the inning.

As Salem was coming off the field I made a few final throws in the bullpen. I grabbed a drink of water and used a towel to wipe my face and arms down. I did the customary fist pound to all the pitchers in the bullpen before I took the field. I stopped for a second, took a deep breath and then headed to the center of the diamond. It was finally the ninth inning and according to my schedule for the evening, I was due to pitch. The whole evening came down to this. It was show time for me on the mound.

Chapter 9
Stay in the Moment: Play Pitch to Pitch

"Don't let yesterday use up too much of today."
- Cherokee Indian Proverb

"No yesterdays are ever wasted for those who give themselves to today."-
Brendan Francis

Everything had gone as planned so far in the game. We had built a 4-0 lead thanks in large part to the two home runs by Gio and the outstanding pitching by Coop. Everything was in place for a Mudcat victory, and all we had to do was record these last three outs. Sounds simple enough right? Any baseball player, pitchers especially, will tell you that the last three outs are the toughest ones to get in baseball. Pair that up with the fact that anyone who knows me would attest, things don't always go as planned when I'm around. Based on those two things, the fans in attendance for this 9th inning were in for a treat.

As I was on the mound throwing my warm up pitches the position changes were announced to the crowd. I didn't listen much to who was where until I heard "and now pitching Justin Toole." With that, the crowd started to make some noise. Anyone who has ever performed in front of a crowd knows that when the crowd gets going, you get going as well. After my last warm up pitch I took a little walk around the mound and grabbed the rosin bag to get rid of the sweat on my arm and hand. I then took a deep breath, got on the mound, and looked in for the sign.

The first batter of the inning was Salem's centerfielder Brandon Jacobs. He was the cleanup hitter for them and hadn't had a hit in his three previous at bats. As he stepped in the box, I got my sign from my catcher and delivered a first pitch fastball for a called strike. You hear people sometimes use the phrase "like riding a bike." Once you learn how to ride a bike you'll always know how to. Pitching in this game was kind of like that for me. Once the umpire put the ball in play it was like I was back out on the mound in high school or college. Up in the count, I got my sign and delivered a curveball. As the pitch approached home plate I saw Jacobs put a good swing on the ball and lucky for me, he skied it into right field.

When Jacobs hit the ball high in the air to right I immediately let out a sigh of relief. He hit it high enough that I knew our rightfielder would be able to get under it without a problem. Now, remember how I said I wasn't paying attention to the position changes when they were announced to the crowd? Well to my complete shock, I turned into right field to see Rob Nixon, the pitcher from the previous inning turning from side to side trying to get himself under the fly ball. I wasn't aware of it when the inning started, but with the game being close, our coaching staff put Rob out into right field in case I got into trouble. That way they could bring him back in the game and finish it off if he needed to. Somehow after all of the circles and turning about that he was doing while trying to figure out where the ball was coming down, he made the catch. It didn't look easy by any means, but he got the job done and recorded the first out of the inning.

Getting that first out of that inning out the way was huge. With one down, Drew Hedman stepped up to the plate. Drew had a base hit earlier in the night to go along with two strikeouts courtesy of Jordan Cooper. The first pitch to him was a ball. I got the ball back and took a deep breath to regroup, and then I fired the next pitch for a strike. With a one and one count the next two pitches I threw were out of the zone. I stepped off the mound and tried to regroup once again, took a deep breath, and got back on the mound. Down in the count three balls and one strike, I had to deliver a pitch in the zone. I did just that, but unlucky for me, Hedman was expecting it. He timed my fastball up perfectly and crushed it. He took my 3-1 pitch and hit it off the scoreboard in right center for a home run.

I remember watching the ball sail out of the park hoping that it would hit off the top of the wall or something. As the ball went over I looked around at my teammates and my eyes made their way over to the bullpen where I saw the bullpen pitchers laughing hysterically. There's always this little rivalry with hitters and pitchers. They think they can hit better than position players can and position players think they can pitch much better than pitchers can. Prior to the game I was guilty of running my mouth a little bit about my pitching ability, and with the latest developments in the 9th inning, the pitchers in the bullpen just couldn't help themselves.

With our lead now just 4-1, I tried to focus in on the next hitter, Sean Coyle. My first pitch after giving up the home run was a ball. The next pitch was also a ball. I definitely didn't want to walk a guy and give him a free pass, so I took a deep breath and delivered the next pitch, a strike. Up to this point I had thrown a lot of fastballs, but when you fall behind in the count that's kind of what you have to do. Down in the count two balls and one strike, I threw Coyle yet another fastball. Much like Hedman, the batter before, Coyle was ready for it and crushed it down the line. This one wasn't hit off the scoreboard; instead it was off the left field foul pole for another home run.

As the ball made its way into left field I kept talking to myself, telling the ball to go foul. When it finally hit the pole I put the glove over my face and kind of laughed to myself. This couldn't possibly be happening, could it? I peeked over at our bullpen again, and found our pitchers were laughing even harder than they were on the first homer. I then glanced at my teammates in the field and many of them had their glove over their faces as well. As I looked to the umpire for a new ball I saw our pitching coach Scott Erickson coming out of the dugout to talk to me.

Prior to the game I had told Scott that he needed to come make a mound visit to talk to me. When I told him that, I didn't imagine giving up back-to-back home runs that would result in him coming out. Once to the mound Scott kind of chuckled and told me to quit throwing fastballs. He suggested maybe trying to throw my curveball or change up. In high school and college my curveball was probably my best pitch. Most of my strikeouts in my pitching career came on that pitch, and so I decided I would take his advice and give it a try. It doesn't hurt having a guy like Scott Erickson giving you pitching advice. His Major League pitching career speaks for itself. As Scott returned to the dugout and everyone took to their positions, I took one last deep breath and got on the mound determined to close the game out.

With one out and our current lead of only 4-2, David Renfroe stepped to the plate. Like Scott told me, I gave him a heavy dose of off speed pitches. The first pitch I threw was for a called strike. He then fouled the next pitch off and I found myself up in the count no balls and two strikes. The next pitch I fired was a ball. I regrouped and then with a 1-2 count, I threw a good curveball that was down in the zone. Renfroe took a good swing, but swung right over the top of it. The ball hit the dirt and DC did a great job of blocking it and getting it to Gio, who was playing first base this inning, for the second out of the 9th inning.

The crowd was really into the game when the inning started, but after the back to back home runs I gave up, their energy was gone and it was pretty quiet. My first strikeout of the evening kind of woke everyone back up and they were on their feet cheering again. We were one out away from closing the game out and I definitely didn't want to let the score get any closer than I already had.

With two outs, David Chester came up for Salem. Chester had a hit earlier in the night and the last thing I wanted to do was give him his second one of the evening. I continued with the heavy dose of off speed pitches, and got a swinging strike for strike one. Chester barely got a piece of my second pitch and fouled it off. I was up early, no balls and two strikes, when I delivered another off speed pitch. Chester took that pitch for a ball. It looked kind of like he was expecting an off speed pitch, since that's all I had thrown since giving up the home runs. Looking in at DC for the sign, I thought maybe a fastball would fool him based on how he reacted to the last pitch I just threw him. DC must have been thinking the same thing because he then called for a fastball outside. The crowd was on their feet clapping in rhythm waiting for that last called strike and final out of the game. I reached back and threw the best fastball I could. Chester definitely didn't see it coming and it froze him. The pitch was right on the outside corner of the plate, and Jansen didn't hesitate to call it for strike three. It was my second strikeout of the inning, but more importantly, it was the third and final out of the ninth inning. The game was over. We had defeated the Salem Red Sox 4-2.

Once the last pitch was called a strike the crowd went crazy. With each strike to the last batter, the crowd got louder and louder. One of my teammates mentioned that it was one of the loudest environments he had ever played in at the moment of that last out. My teammates rushed onto the field and there was a big congratulatory celebration on the pitcher's mound. The feeling I had was one of relief with a huge sense of achievement. I was more proud than anything to have assured the victory for our team, but the way it happened couldn't have gone any better than it did. Well, maybe except for those two home runs by Hedman and Coyle.

That feeling I had when the last pitch was delivered was one I will never ever forget. Too often in my career I hadn't taken the chance to enjoy moments when I probably should have. When I was in high school, I was always serious about trying to get better and worrying about trying to get a scholarship to a D-I college. When I was in college, I was always thinking about playing professionally and what I needed to do to get better in order to do that. Not that I didn't enjoy my high school and college experiences, but I feel like I didn't enjoy the moment as much as I should have at certain times. I was always looking forward to the next camp or the next game. As I mentioned, something I have learned as I have gotten older is to stay in the moment and enjoy it. As I've said throughout this entire book, not only has that lesson helped me to grow as a player, but it has also helped me grow as a person. On this particular night, I definitely embraced the whole experience and enjoyed the moment as much as I could.

The baseball term that people use when talking about staying in the moment is playing pitch to pitch. Playing pitch to pitch means you are focused in on the current pitch and are not worried about anything else. You aren't worried about previous pitches and you aren't looking ahead to future pitches. Once a pitch is done and over with, you move on to the next one, and so on. What playing pitch to pitch does for you as a player is it locks you into the now, the current moment. It gets your mind ready to compete and with a clear head you allow your body to work. Travis Fryman used to always say his old manager, Charlie Manuel, would tell him "empty head full bat, full head empty bat." If you think about that, it makes complete sense.

People who have standout performances in athletics will sometimes tell you they couldn't remember what they were thinking during an amazing performance in a game. The reason for that is they weren't thinking about anything other than what was going on at that present moment. That's the goal for every athlete every time they take the floor or step out on the field. It's definitely not easy to do, but you can do it with a lot of practice and the right mindset. That's what sports psychology is all about. It's about taking that one game and that one amazing performance and breaking it down so that you can understand what you were thinking and doing in order for you to be able to repeat it and have it happen more often in your career.

The top of the ninth inning was a great example of what happens when people play pitch to pitch. I went from having one of the worst things that could happen to a pitcher, giving up back-to-back home runs, to having the one of the most enjoyable things that happens to a pitcher, striking someone out to end a game. My ability didn't change at all between those different hitters; the only thing that changed was my mind set and how I executed pitches. I didn't get caught up in the fact that two guys crushed balls to the moon off me, I just put it behind me and focused on the next task at hand. A lot of people will call that damage control. Too often, when a pitcher starts to go bad, he lets things snowball on him. People who stay in the moment and put the past behind them, allow themselves a chance to stay out of a big inning and keep the snowballing to a minimum.

Just because one shot doesn't go in, just because you strikeout, or just because you walk someone doesn't mean that you can't have success on the very next pitch or attempt. The best players in the world are the ones who can separate the past and not let what's already happened to them affect their future. There is a great quote that is up in the weight room of the Cleveland Indians Player Development Complex in Arizona where we have spring training. The quote is by Hall of Famer Bob Feller. The quote reads, "Every day is a new opportunity. You can build on yesterday's success or put its failures behind and start over again. That's the way life is, with a new game every day, and that's the way baseball is." Feller's quote is spot on. One failed attempt won't lead to another failed attempt, just as one successful attempt doesn't mean the next attempt will be successful. If you have success, try and build on it, but if you don't, don't let it bother you and keep on moving forward.

Many athletes who play high school baseball want to play in college and most everyone who plays in college wants to play professionally. Don't get so caught up in trying to reach the next level that you don't enjoy where you are at right now. Like I said earlier in this book, if you take care of right now, your future will pan out just like you want. If you're in high school, enjoy the ride. Enjoy competing with your teammates, the bus rides, and all of the memories you make. If you're in college, enjoy the spring break trips to warm places, the conference tournaments, the long bus rides and plane trips, and if you're lucky enough to participate in it, enjoy the NCAA Tournament and the College World Series. You only get one chance to experience these kinds of things, so take full advantage of it.

When you focus in on playing pitch to pitch or staying in the moment, you will find yourself having more success and playing at a much higher level. Enjoying the moment doesn't mean messing around and not taking things serious, it just means you're locked into your current task and nothing else. As I have said before, my best seasons have happened when I enjoyed and stayed in the moment, compared to other seasons where I have been worried about too many other things instead of what was most important, the task at hand.

Now that the game was over, and with a Mudcats victory, I could cross the last two parts of my checklist off. Base hit, check. Playing errorless and good defense, check. Mudcats victory, check. I think if you had told me how the game was going to play out and what was going to happen before the game started, I probably wouldn't have believed it. The fans were awesome the whole game. I owe a big thank you to the 5,958 fans (according to the official attendance numbers) that were there for the entire game. Hopefully you all enjoyed a cool experience and a fun game. My teammates played well, and most importantly we won the game.

Salem finished the game with two runs on eight hits, while committing one error. We finished with four runs, on only five hits, while committing no errors. Miguel Celestino was credited with the loss while Jordan Cooper picked up the win, his eighth of the season.

The game seemed to fly by once it started and the official time of the game was a quick two hours and eleven minutes. It was an amazing experience and I couldn't be more thankful to have gotten an opportunity to do what I did on that special night. Not many people can ever say they successfully played nine positions in one nine inning game, but I'm lucky enough to say I've done it.

I wouldn't have been able to accomplish this feat if it wasn't for the awesome people who allowed for it to happen. I want to thank all of those who made this night possible and anyone who was involved in any way. Thanks to my teammates, my coaching staff, the fans, the Carolina Mudcats, the Cleveland Indians Organization, the Salem Red Sox, all of the media who picked up the game, and anyone else who was a part of this special night. It was definitely the highlight of my career, and a night that I will never forget.

REFERENCES
(Info references I used that helped make this book possible)

Chapter 4
http://www.history.com/this-day-in-history/gehrig-ends-streak
http://www.baseball-almanac.com/quotes/quogehr.shtml
http://www.baseball-almanac.com/quotes/quopipp.shtml
(Wally Pipp, Lou Gehrig Info)

Chapter 5
http://www.ncaa.org/wps/wcm/connect/public/Test/Issues/Recruiting/
Probability+of+Going+Pro
(NCAA Chart)

Chapter 6
http://bleacherreport.com/articles/1165882-the-25-best-undrafted-
free-agent-signings-in-nfl-history
http://mlb.mlb.com/news/article.jsp?ymd=20100624&content_id=115
32374&fext=.jsp&c_id=mlb
(Undrafted and Free Agent Player Info)

Entire Book
http://www.milb.com/gameday/index.jsp?gid=2012_08_25_salafa_cm
cafa_1
http://www.milb.com/milb/stats/stats.jsp?sid=t414&gid=2012_08_25_
salafa_cmcafa_1&cid=414&t=g_box
(Game Info, Carolina Mudcats vs. Salem Red Sox, August 25, 2012)

Special "Thank You" to the following for their help in putting together this book:

Lee Toole
Jeanine Toole
Brian Cain
Justin Dedman
Angela Hoy
Todd Engel
Booklocker.com, Inc.
Darren Headrick
Tom Miller
Nikolaus Johnson
FedEx
NCAA
Carolina Mudcats
Cleveland Indians
Lorna Woods
Joan Cooling-Noeller
Jenny Schuelke

CPSIA information can be obtained
at www.ICGtesting.com
Printed in the USA
FFOW04n1546271116